Hector Ó hEochagáin became a household name following the runaway success of his series of offbeat travel programmes on TG4.

Other series, including *Only Fools Buy Horses* and *Hanging with Hector*, have secured his place as one of the most popular broadcasters in the country. Hector lives in Galway with his wife and two children.

HECTOR'S WORLD

On the Road with Ireland's Favourite Redhead

Pare mí Padre, the oul fella,
mo dhaidí, a proud Navanman,
who loved Meath football.
I hope this makes you laugh !.!

PENGUIN IRELAND

Published by the Penguin Group

Penguin Ireland, 25 St Stephen's Green, Dublin 2, Ireland
(a division of Penguin Books Ltd)

Penguin Books Ltd, 80 Strand, London WC2R 0RL, England

Penguin Group (USA) Inc., 375 Hudson Street, New York, New York 10014, USA

Penguin Group (Canada), 90 Eglinton Avenue East,
Suite 700, Toronto, Ontario, Canada M4P 2Y3
(a division of Pearson Penguin Canada Inc.)

Penguin Group (Australia), 250 Camberwell Road,
Camberwell, Victoria 3124, Australia (a division
of Pearson Australia Group Pty Ltd)

Penguin Books India Pvt Ltd, 11 Community Centre,
Panchsheel Park, New Delhi – 110 017, India

Penguin Group (NZ), cnr Airborne and Rosedale Roads, Albany, Auckland 1310,
New Zealand
(a division of Pearson New Zealand Ltd)

Penguin Books (South Africa) (Pty) Ltd,
24 Sturdee Avenue, Rosebank,
Johannesburg 2196, South Africa

Penguin Books Ltd, Registered Offices: 80 Strand,
London WC2R 0RL, England

www.penguin.com

First published 2006
1

Copyright © Hector Ó hEochagáin, 2006

ISBN-13: 978-1-844-881109
ISBN-10: 1-844-881105

All photographs taken on location by TG4 unless otherwise stated

Reportage photography by Chris Terry. Pages 2-3, 9, 70-71,
119, 253, 256. Copyright © Chris Terry, 2006

Still life photography by Dan Duchars. Pages 1, 69, 73, 104-105,
114-115, 116, 118, 158, 164-167, 195, 210, 214, 218.
Copyright © Dan Duchars, 2006

All pack-shots by Foto Theme Digital Ltd.
Pages 45, 80, 98, 129, 138, 159, 198-199, 200, 203.
Copyright © Foto Theme Digital Ltd, 2006

The publishers & author would also like to thank the following for the use
of additional images: John Hamilton (page 50), Nathan Burton (page 56-57),
Sophie Dangerfield & Richard Durham (pages 133 & 139).

Illustrations by Dominic Trevett. Pages 14, 17, 18, 21.
Copyright © Dominic Trevett, 2006

Every effort has been made to trace copyright holders and we apologize
in advance for any unintentional omission. We would be pleased to insert
appropriate acknowledgement in any subsequent editions.

The publishers & author would also like to thank *Paperchase* for their assistance

Set in Solex and Impact

Printed in Great Britain by Dot Gradations Ltd

A CIP catalogue record for this book is available from
the British Library

HOW IT ALL STARTED . . .

IN THE SUMMER OF 1979, my mother enrolled me in Coláiste na bhFiann for the first time. This was hardcore Irish College. There was an entrance interview (I lied about my age: you had to be ten to get in, and I was nine), plus you had to know all the words of 'Amhrán na bhFiann'. The entire coláiste assembled every morning to sing it and raise the flag. Besides classes, there was a big emphasis on the culture. We played sports in the afternoon and there was a céili every evening. One sentence of Béarla and you were out the door. The first day of the cúrsa nearly always coincided with the men's singles final in Wimbledon. I remember one time, this girl sang out, 'Does anyone know if McEnroe won?' Never saw her again.

You even courted through Irish.

'An rachaidh tú amach liom?'

'Sea.'

In for the shift.

Every year between 1979 and 1988, I spent the first three weeks of July in Irish College. Here's where I got my grá for the language. Not school - I only got a C in the Leaving. I didn't have to spend ten years way out in the back of beyonds to get it either. It was all in Coláiste na bhFiann, and it all started in Ráth Cairn, the Meath Gaeltacht.

When I got older, they made me a cúntóir, or prefect. You helped organize the games, the dances, the songs. I got my first taste of the performing, teaching 100 thirteen-year-olds stuff like the Ballaí Luimní. It was brilliant. I loved it.

'TWO DAYS LATER I GOT A CALL TO SAY **I'D GOT THE JOB.** THIS WAS CHRISTMAS 1996. MYSELF AND DYMPNA DANCED AROUND THE KITCHEN. I WAS GOING TO HAVE MY OWN SHOW. MY VERY OWN TV SHOW. I THOUGHT I HAD IT MADE. I THOUGHT IT'D BE ALL RED CARPETS, PERSONAL WARDROBE CONSULTANTS AND FERRERO ROCHER FROM THEN ON.

I WAS BACK ON THE DOLE IN THREE MONTHS.

The television career started with a sign, posted on a notice board in GMIT. 'Teilifís na Gaeilge ag oscailt go gairid. An bhfuil suim agat bheith í do láithreoir teilifíse? Anyone interested should come to…' A mate of mine, Maggie, spotted it and showed it to Dympna (the 'missus'). 'Hector should do this.' Hector was a year and a half back from the Basque Country, on the dole, spending most of his time either drinking pints or playing the slots out in Salthill.

I had no car, so I got my mate Axel to drive me out to the audition in his. It was in a big warehouse out in Indreabhán in Connemara. Myself and six others standing around nervously waiting to see what would happen. They told us that it was a fashion programme, called *Íomhá*, due to air just as soon as the new station was up and running. Inside, they had a mock studio set-up. You had to get out in front of camera, introduce yourself and talk for three minutes on a particular fashion topic – all as Gaeilge of course. The topics they had written on little scraps of paper scrunched up and mixed together inside a glass box. You pulled one out and had ten minutes to figure out what you were going to say.

I slowly uncurled the little scrap of paper in my hand. Fake tans. Shite. What the hell did I know about fake tans? While I was struggling to think of something to say, I could see Axel outside, making faces in the window at me.

In the end I just turned the thing on its head and started talking about freckles, about redheads and sunburn and the rest of it.

Two days later I got a call to say I'd got the job. This was Christmas 1996. Myself and Dympna danced around the kitchen. I was going to have my own show. My very own TV show. I thought I had it made. I thought it'd be all red carpets, personal wardrobe consultants and Ferrero Rocher from then on.

I was back on the dole in three months.

Over the next four years, I got a few more TV gigs, but most of the time, it was a case of trying to pick up a few squid here and there. I did everything from painting houses to pressing clothes in Shannon Dry Cleaners. Christmas of 1997, I hadn't a penny. I borrowed some money, went down to the garden centre and bought 100 terracotta pots, stuffed them with pine cones and candles, then tied them up with tartan ribbon and sold the lot in the market for £15 each. Tommy Tiernan bought one. A couple of years ago, just after we'd finished the third series of the show, myself and Dympna were down in Tralee for the Rose. A guy came up to me on the street. 'Hector, is it true, right, that your show, it's just you and your mates go off on holiday and take a camera? Is that right, yeah? You just sent it in to TG4 and they liked it. Is that true?' Another time, I did a telephone interview with an Irish magazine. They had another story. Apparently, there were so many applications, the producers couldn't decide. Then, at this final brainstorming session, where they had to pick a presenter, somebody kicked a filing cabinet and my picture floated gently on to the desk like an autumn leaf. 'Him! He's the guy! Call him!'

The truth is boring by comparison.

Early in 2000, I got a call from Adare Productions. They were working on a new series. Ten shows, to be shot over seven weeks in the US, interviewing Irish-speakers in quirky jobs. Would I audition?

Arrah, yeah, sure I'll think about it.

It was a funny kind of audition. Up in Monkstown, out on the street. They got Christine from the office to pretend to be a soldier in Cherry Point Marine Base, where the first show in the series was going to be shot. It started raining as we got going. Cars were beeping at us. I had to introduce the programme, interview your one, then wrap the thing up. After the opening spiel, I turned to Christine and said something like, well, you're the best-looking marine I ever saw . . .

Before I got home on the train that night, they'd rung Dympna to say I got the job. We danced around the kitchen **again.**

We had different production teams in the first two series, to America and Europe. Rónan Ó Donnchadha did an amazing job producing *Amú le Hector*, the one that brought us from Fossett's Circus to the Playboy Mansion by way of Bollywood and Memphis. Rónan's a passionate Yellowbelly and a great singer. At a karaoke night in Wet Willie's in Memphis, we were the only white people in the place. Didn't stop Rónan from getting up and bringing the house down with his version of 'Let's Get It On'. On the way out, the bouncer told him he wasn't bad for a honky.

But it was on the Asian trip – the first really big one – that myself, Evan and Rosco were thrown together for the first time: Evan Chamberlain the producer and Ross O'Callaghan the cameraman. Before the twelve-hour flight to Bangkok, we'd only spent an hour in each other's company.

First impressions were poor, especially of Rosco. He arrived into the airport wearing a rugby shirt with the collar turned up. Then on the flight, he took out a Michael Schumacher biography. Oh for fuck's sake, I was thinking. I have to live in this fool's pocket for the next three months. A couple of hours into the flight, the slagging started, and after the first round of beers, he threw away the book. By the time we landed, I had a pain in my face from laughing.

I'll never forget the sense of excitement heading off that first day. Flicking through that twenty-page itinerary, reading down through the list of flights.and cities. Bangkok, Ho Chi Minh, Kyoto, Manila . . . Here we were, three lads off to Asia with a camera to shoot thirteen TV programmes over thirteen weeks. No one looking over our shoulder, no one checking up on us.

I'd never been to Asia before. The place is like another planet. It's hot and loud and packed and just so intensely alive. That first night in Bangkok, we went out to get something to eat and stopped at this rough little streetside bar all decked out in Christmas-tree lights. Three hours later, Evan was standing on the counter, singing Boyzone into a sweeping brush.

It could have been a disaster, it could have ended in tears, but over those three months, we became as close as brothers. In all that time, and through the trips that followed it, we never had one cross word. I think if I had to pinpoint one reason why the shows worked so well, that would be it.

A lot of the time, the only trouble is trying to get the laughing under control so I can do my piece to camera. It doesn't matter where we are in the world, how wrecked we are, how shitty the transport or the accommodation, one of the boys will say or do something, we'll fall around laughing, and that's it. Everyone's in great form, and the work goes perfectly.

Evan is Mr Professional. He works his arse off. While myself and Rosco are dossing by the pool the day after we arrive, he's off meeting his contacts, organizing visas and permits, setting up interviews. Rosco meanwhile would tie the camera round his ankle and hang out of a jumbo jet to get the right shot. And he always gets the right shot.

REPÚBLICA DE VENEZUELA
(201-828)

16 ABR 2002

AEROPUERTO INTERNACIONAL
SIMON BOLIVAR

ENTRADA

VENEZUELA
(201-635)

21 ABR 2002

The best bit is just after we finish something and he looks up from the camera. 'Hector, wait 'til you see this. Have a look at this.' I just love it when he says that. He sticks a fag in the corner of his mouth and lights up. Evan comes running over, and we all crowd round the camera.

'That's class,' says Evan

Rosco takes a pull of the fag.

'Class.'

It's been an amazing experience, taking the Irish language all over the world, whether it's singing Sean Nós in the Amazon jungle, interviewing Irish cops in New York or pricing a blowjob in Amsterdam. These shows would never have worked as Béarla, if only because you can get away with murder when you're talking Irish.

You'll hear everyone at it these days. Talking Irish. I even get 'Dia dhuit, Hector' from the Filipino women at the coffee shop in the airport. TG4 have been at the centre of this revival. You don't have to be a native speaker, you don't have to speak a word of the language to enjoy it. It's just great programming, start to finish.

Without TG4, I wouldn't have a career in TV. More importantly, I probably wouldn't have made it on to the Leaving Cert Irish paper.

We had the best crack ever making these shows. We had experiences that I'll never forget. Here are the funniest, the weirdest, the scariest, the best stories from the last six years.

Bainigí taitneamh as,

Meas Mór,

Hector

ALASKA
GREENLAND
CANADA
An dig mór
Don't forget your sock
GET your kit off!!!
UNITED STATES OF AMERICA
CHICAGO
Boston
NEW YORK
full of D'Irish
Coolest city in America
SAN FRANCISCO
HEFNER'S WORLD
(full of bunnies)
Viva
LAS VEGAS
ZZZ!
TENNESSEE
Yihaw!!
NASHVILLE
MEMPHIS
PASADENA
LOS ANGELES
SAN FERNANDO VALLEY
Southfork
DALLAS
NEW BERN
HOOOOORAH!
HECTOR!
LA FRONTERA
Y'all come back now ya' hear!
MEXICO
SPEEDY
Gonzalez
ARIBA
ARIBA!
CUBA
JAMAICA
MEXICO CITY
Mucho miedo!
PACIFIC OCEAN
NORTH AMERICA

ASIA

RUSSIA

MONGOLIA

CHINA

INDIA

SRI LANKA

Yum Yum Beetles!

We ♥ boy bands

BEIJING

Seoul

JAPAN
crazy neon future land

TOKYO
Narita Airport never again!

KYOTO

HIROSHIMA

leather hotpants

Buachailli + Cailini O

BANGKOK

Lady boy

TAIPEI

TAIWAN
DR TU!

Some Lad to go!

Shizzha...
Shizzha!
shizzha !!

skg

HONG KONG

Kuala Lumpur

Cu Chi Tunnels

HO CHI MINH

MANILA

PHILIPPINES

PACIFIC OCEAN

$ $ $
BRUNEI $

SUMATRA

SINGAPORE

Milton keynes of Asia

BORNEO

INDONESIA

INDIAN OCEAN

BALI
OH MO THOIN!!

cool!

AUSTRALIA

ICELAND

minke whale with Rainbow Warrior boys

And here are the votes from the Norwegian area: DEUX POINTS!

NORWAY

SWEDEN

4 DAYS too long!!!

HELSINKI

MOSCOW

BALTIC SEA

RUSSIA

red arrows

COPENHAGEN

Uri Geller

My Hector baby!

BERLIN

The Dubliners

NAVAN

centre of the known universe

Mi casa

SASANNA

NOTTINGHAM

Big mad airport

AN BAILE

Witches Wooo!!

HASTINGS

"THE DAM"

peace bed

VIENNA

"♫ I've been a wild rover for manys a year... ♫"

QUIMPER

No Mans Land

DEL PIERO LAND

LOURDES

BILBAO

PAMPLONA

AUPA EUSICAOi!

ATLANTIC OCEAN

MEDITERRANEAN SEA

EUROPE

AFRICA

SWEAT

FUN & DERMATITIS IN FIVE OF THE WORLD'S HOTTEST HOTSPOTS

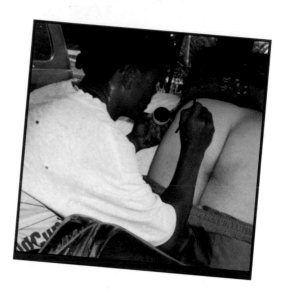

BALI

GOD KNOWS THERE ARE BETTER WAYS TO SPEND YOUR AFTERNOON THAN BENT OVER THE BACK SEAT OF A CRAMPED AND STUFFY 1981 HIACE WITH A SHORT BALINESE FLIP-FLOP SELLER TATTOOING YOUR ARSE. BUT I AM A PROFESSIONAL. IF THE SHOW DEMANDS A TATTOOED ARSE, A TATTOOED ARSE IS WHAT THE SHOW WILL GET.

Bali. The third stop on our Asian tour. The story was mainly in the beaches, the bars, the drugs and the surfing Australians, though we went inland too. In Ubud we had some decent footage of me making a pig's arse of a traditional Balinese dance. On the drive up, we came across an unlicensed cockfight, but it was fairly hard on the stomach, so in the end we decided not to use it.

The thing was, we needed a good ending. You always need a good beginning and a good ending – what they call an intro and an outro. We had the intro. Rosco had been hauling an underwater camera bag around with him since we left Dublin, but it wasn't until we got to Bali that he got an excuse to use it. For that opening scene, he strapped the camera across a surfboard, and, with the water sparkling in the lens, I walked out from the shore doing the introduction.

We couldn't come up with a decent outro until, on day three, the two boys came back from the beach with henna tattoos. Now, as everybody knows, henna tattoos are for transition-year schoolgirls and no one else. But here's Evan, a big, strapping Mountbellew man, with a little dragon on his bicep. He even picked up a singlet on the beach to show the thing off. Rosco has this ring of barbed wire on his arm. Ah for Jaysus sake, lads, I said when I saw them. But this is the inspiration for the closing sequence. As the sun set on the clear blue waters of Pacific, I would do my piece to camera – Slán o Bali and see you next week! – then strip off the shirt, turn towards the surf and drop

the fobhrístí to reveal the words 'Amú San Áise' tattooed on the cheeks. So far as we knew, it would be the first Irish-language TV henna ass tattoo.

Finding the right man for the job wasn't exactly difficult. Kuta beach, a surfer's paradise on the south Balinese coast, has more henna tattooists per square inch than anywhere in the world. Freddie, it would turn out, had been in the business less than a month.

Three weeks earlier, Freddie had been what you'd loosely call the 'transportation manager' of a big counterfeiting outfit on one of the neighbouring islands. Each Saturday morning himself and his cousin Jally would cross the short channel from the island in his uncle's 14-foot boat, laden with fake designer flip-flops destined for the soles of the western feet. When the cops started cracking down on designer rip-offs, Freddie decided to get out of flip-flops and into henna tattoos until the heat died down.

We told him we'd pay double for an unusual job. We couldn't do it on the beach, though. For one thing, there were privacy considerations, but more importantly, there was the risk of a scorching. Apart from maybe a brief flash in Bettystown in the summer of 1976, when it came to the sun, this was virgin flesh . . . Freddie grinned and shrugged. He asked no questions. Nor did he flinch when eventually confronted with **two prime cuts of Navan rump steak.** *Dollars were dollars, and the children had to eat.*

Privacy was our decrepit Hiace. There used to be hundreds of vans like this on Irish roads. Twenty-five years old, on its third circuit of the clock, held together with chewing gum and Sellotape. Green, with one maroon door. Coathanger aerial. Inside, the seats were like the ones they used to have in the Falcon Bar in Navan. Shit-coloured leather all torn and patched with masking tape. Big chunks of foam leaking out of it. Dartha, our ever-grinning driver, picked us up from the airport in this museum piece. 'Harrrrrmony! Harrrrrmony!' said Dartha as we stood staring at this thing in the airport car park. We'd just come down from Singapore, where it was hot, but not half as hot as this. 'I don't suppose she's air conditioning?' I asked him. 'Harrrrrrrmony! Harrrrrrmony!' said Dartha, pulling back the maroon door. 'Don't worry about heat!' Inside, six Irish thighs welded instantly to the tattered upholstery.

Two days later I'm bent over the same upholstery while Evan explains the job to Freddie. 'Amú, that's A, M, U, with a fada over the U.' He's writing it out on a bit of paper. 'That now, that's a fada, got it? Now we want that there on that cheek, see? Big and black as you can get it. Then here, right, on the other one, we want San Áise. S A N and new word, A I S E. Another fada over the A. Right?' Freddie beams and nods, like this happens every day. I half expect him to say he had Miriam O'Callaghan in the other week, getting Prime Time done.

The two boys head off to get some lunch, leaving myself and Freddie alone in the van. He's all scrunched up down in the back where the children sit, squatting in the tightest, most uncomfortable spot in Bali while my pale blue tóin hovers above him. It's at this point that the extreme vulnerability of the position I've adopted suddenly hits home. 'So, Freddie,' I turn the head back. 'Tell us, are you married or what?' Freddie looks up from his work and beams back at me. 'Married with four children!' Good man, Freddie. Lean ar aghaidh.

Two hours. Two hours of sweat and cramps and about half a gallon of henna. We'd parked the van in the car park of the Hard Rock Café just up from the beach. Not the most secluded spot in the world. As Freddie sweated away in the back, I watched the surfer girls go by outside. Occasionally, one of them would look over, do a double take and nudge her mates. 'Dia Dhaoibh a cailíní! Conas atá sibh?' Evan would reappear every so often to laugh, take pictures and make sure the fadas were going where they should be. 'It's going to be great! It's going to be great!' he kept saying. 'Now we're going swimming, see you in a while.' When Freddie eventually crawled out from the back seat, crippled with pins and needles, I still had a ways to go. He'd used so much henna, the thing was going to take another two hours to dry. There was all this building work going on up on the roof of the café, but the boys got nothing done that afternoon. They kept coming back to the edge to have another look at this ginger-headed Irishman, standing between the van and the wall with the shirt in his teeth and the shorts around his ankles. One smudge and the whole afternoon would be down the toilet.

THE TWO BOYS HEAD OFF TO GET SOME LUNCH, LEAVING MYSELF AND FREDDIE ALONE IN THE VAN. HE'S ALL SCRUNCHED UP DOWN IN THE BACK WHERE THE CHILDREN SIT, **SQUATTING IN THE TIGHTEST, MOST UNCOMFORTABLE SPOT IN BALI WHILE MY PALE BLUE TÓIN HOVERS ABOVE HIM.**

Evan picks up a sarong at one of the stalls that run alongside the beach and I get my David Beckham moment waddling down to the shore with it wrapped around Freddie's artwork.

Piece to camera, shirt off, turn round, drop sarong. There it is. Amú San Áise. Each letter boldly inscribed on the twin orbs of my Navan arse. It is with a sense of professional satisfaction that I bound gazelle-like into the waves and dive into the crystal waters. Perfect. Or it would have been if Evan hadn't added his own twist. I turn back to the shore to see him tearing off up the beach with my clothes. An hour later I'm still standing hip-deep in the sea, waiting for the bastard to come back. It's only out of a sense of diplomacy and sensitivity to the local population that I don't emerge from the water to inflict the ginger pubes and the Golden Buddha on them.

Postscript

We're in Asia now and everything's cheaper. The Taipei Sheraton is one class hotel and costs only a fraction of what you'd pay in the west. Ten days after we leave Bali, we're on a day off before shooting the Taiwan show. I'm about to have a wash and put on a clean shirt before heading into town. Walking into the mirrored shower, I catch sight of the arse. 'Holy Jesus, what the fuck is that?' The henna's gone. Not a screed of it remains. But the letters are still there. Amú San Áise, plain as day. No longer inscribed in henna but in a **RAW RED RASH** rising up out of the skin. Tentatively, I reach round and touch the E. Rough, like bark. I run my finger up and down it. It's like Braille. You can read the whole thing, no bother, without seeing it. 'Oh, Holy Jesus ... Boys! Get in here and have a look at this!' Evan and Rosco, surprise surprise, fail to grasp the seriousness of the situation. It takes the pair of them about fifteen minutes to control the laughing.

The hotel doctor on the sixteenth floor is open for business between nine a.m. and two p.m. He takes one look at it - and not a very long look for some reason - and refers me to the dermatology clinic in the Municipal Jen-Ai Hospital downtown.

These guys do hospitals the way hospitals should be done. Surgically clean and white as snow. Nobody on trolleys. They put me in this little treatment room and eventually the dermatologist shows up. Short woman in her mid-thirties. 'OK,' she says, 'what is problem?'

I stand up, unbuckle the belt and turn round. 'This,' I tell her, lowering the fobhrístí yet again, 'is the name of my TV show.'

'Ooooookay,' says she, pulling on the latex gloves. A tender poke. 'Hmmmmmm . . . Sore?'

'Ah . . . Not really.'

'Itch?'

'Yeah, a bit.'

I hear the squeak and slap of gloves being removed again. 'OK. Pants up.'

She gives me a prescription for this high-strength steroid cream, and I pick up four tubs of the stuff on the way back to the hotel. It does the trick. By the time we get back to Ireland three months later the rash has faded completely, leaving these cute little black hairs that still spell out the name of the show.

>*MAM:* WHY DID YOU GET THE NAME OF YOUR *SHOW* TATTOOED ON YOUR BOTTOM?

>**HECTOR:** *Mam,* **because it was funny,** *Mam.*

>*MAM:* It was **NOT** funny now, it was **NOT** funny.

>**HECTOR:** Ah, Mam . . .

>*MAM:* Doing that dance that you did, **NOW THAT** WAS FUNNY, I laughed at that, but showing your bottom, *your painted bottom* to the world, now that wasn't funny.

>**HECTOR:** MAM . . .

>*MAM: Why do you keep* **taking off your clothes?**

>**HECTOR:** I DON'T **KEEP** TAKING OFF MY CLOTHES, MAM, *IT WAS JUST...*

>*MAM:* I'm half afraid to turn on the television set any more.

>**HECTOR:** *Ah, Mam.*

>*MAM:* No, I am. I don't know what bit of you we'll see next.

>**HECTOR:** MAM, I . . .

>*MAM:* Gay Byrne did the Late Late for thirty years, and you **NEVER** even saw his elbows. *We see more of your bottom than your face.* I can't believe they let it out at that hour of the night. All the kids round here watching it. What kind of example is it to them? They'll all be at it now. THEY'LL ALL BE GOING AROUND WITH THEIR **PENISES OUT.** 'Oh, Hector does it, so it must be OK..'

> **HAVANA FEELS LIKE A SONG.** MUSIC ALL OVER THE STREET, THESE BEAUTIFUL, OLD BUILDINGS FRONTING THE PLAZAS, SOME OF THEM CRUMBLING, SOME RESTORED TO THEIR OLD GLORY. WASHING STRUNG ACROSS WROUGHT-IRON BALCONIES. MEN DRESSED LIKE LATIN GIGOLOS WITH WIDE, OPEN-COLLAR SHIRTS, PULLING ON HUGE CIGARS OR BENT OVER THE BONNETS OF THESE BIG, OLD FIFTIES-ERA CARS.

CUBA

CUBA AND VIETNAM. THE ONLY PLACES IN FIFTY-SIX SHOWS WHERE WE WERE ACCOMPANIED BY GOVERNMENT HANDLERS EVERYWHERE WE WENT. In Cuba, our minder never really got comfortable with us. I spent a lot of time arsing around the streets, having the chat, trying to knock a bit of crack out of whoever was about. Not your straight-up holiday-show fare. The fact that I was talking Irish to the camera was a major headache, of course. For all he knew I could have been telling everyone that Fidel was the son of a one-legged syphilitic whore. After a couple of days, he just gave up and hid out in the back of the van while we went out and did our thing. I did have one argument with him. At La Coppelia, the famous open-air theatre where everyone goes to eat ice-cream in the evenings. They have these stupid rules to keep foreigners and Cubans apart, so there's one queue for locals, one for tourists. I told him I was going to get into the Cuban queue and that he wasn't going to stop me. He had the last laugh. As soon as we broke ranks, the cops were over, wagging their fingers and herding us back in line.

Havana feels like a song. Music all over the street, these beautiful, old buildings fronting the plazas, some of them crumbling, some restored to their old glory. Washing strung across wrought-iron balconies. Men dressed like Latin gigolos with wide, open-collar shirts, pulling on huge cigars or bent over the bonnets of these big, old fifties-era cars. The trade embargo with the US means that you don't get the kinds of brands you see everywhere else in the world. No Burger King, Pizza Hut or McDonald's. All the American cars on the streets date from before the '57 revolution, so they're Oldsmobiles, Chevys and Lincolns.

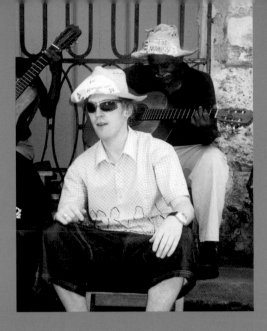

In the evening, the young people get together on the promenade at Malecon and drink cheap Havana Club, watching the sun go down. Friendly, for the most part. I lost track of the number of times I was offered hashish - which they call chocolate (pronounced 'chockolatay') - and women.

If you want to get to know the locals, though, try the paladares before the prostitutes. Another of Fidel's initiatives, families are allowed to open up their homes as restaurants and, so long as the government gets its monthly cut, the family can make a little money on the side. It's a closed society, of course, you forget that. Besides na drúgaí agus na striopachaí, I was approached several times by people looking to buy my passport.

They put us up in the Hotel Nacionale, a huge, rambling old palace that looked like something out of *Bugsy Malone*. Crammed with old black-and-white photos of stars from the forties and fifties: Greta Garbo, Jimmy Cagney, Clark Gable. The first night, we found this brilliant music club, full of people tangoing and salsaing like professionals. You could buy a bottle of seven-year-old Havana Club rum for $4.50 in the club, but one of the locals told us to pick it up at the kiosk outside for $1.50 and smuggle it in. I know it was only three lousy dollars, but I had this flashback to my Feile days. Waddling in to see the Black Crows with about twenty cans down the trousers. Of course, the minute we tried to open the stupid bottle under the table, the guy was over to confiscate it. The mortification.

Before we ever left Ireland for South America, we had a section of the Cuba programme already in the bag. This little cheat was all Fidel's fault. We'd tried to get an interview with Che Guevara's daughter Alieda, but the bureaucracy kept getting in the way. It was on, it was off, it was on... Finally it was off for good. For reasons that the authorities wouldn't explain, they didn't want us talking to her. Then we heard that she was coming to Ireland, to Galway. Che's grandmother, Anna Lynch, was born, they think, somewhere in west Galway before moving to South America in the 1800s. In a handy little coincidence, Alieda was coming to the west to check out her Irish roots. We got in touch and asked her for an interview. No problem, she said, I'd love to.

BEFORE WE LEFT, HE SANG ME A SONG – 'DOS GARDENIAS' – AND SIGNED MY COPY OF THE ALBUM. **'PARA MI AMIGO HECTOR', EXCEPT HE SPELT IT 'HETOR'. 'AMIGOS PARA SIEMPRE'. COOL.** ESPECIALLY POIGNANT NOW THAT HE'S NO LONGER WITH US.

So, on a cold and wintry April day, we met her in the Great Southern on Eyre Square. Rosco, bent over the lens, directed proceedings. 'OK, first thing close the curtains. You can see Roche's Stores out the window. Yeah, and take that picture of the Claddagh off the wall... We're going to have to lose the Ballygowan too, and the Galway Crystal.' Afterwards, I had to make sure I brought the same shirt with me to Cuba. We took lots of general views of me strolling through Havana and, in editing, spread these liberally through the Galway interview. Alieda herself was so soft-spoken you could hardly hear what she was saying. Apart from the fact that she referred to Castro as Uncle Fidel, I can't remember a single thing she said.

We found Ibrahim Ferrer through the sleeve notes on the Buena Vista Social Club album. A Barcelona management company referred us to the studio in Havana where they put the thing together, and they just called him up and said, hey, Ibrahim, fancy talking to an Irish crew? Nothing like the hoo ha in trying to get an interview with Che's daughter. His story, the story of the album, is well known now. These guys played for peanuts all their lives, then, in their seventies, Ry Cooder's recording and Wim Wenders' film made them international superstars.

In he strode dressed in this wild black shirt festooned with flaming suns, a shrunken cabbage-patch-doll face beneath his cap, clutching this little good-luck totem of his, a stick with the carved head of St Lazarus on the end. 'I was at home,' he told me, 'it was three o'clock in the afternoon and Juan de Marcos (one of the band) came looking for me . . . I wasn't too bothered. He said, I've come to see you because I need help with a recording I'm doing. I said I didn't want to record any more. I'd given up singing. I wasn't feeling great. He said, look, you'll make fifty quid . . . That changed things straightaway. I asked him when. Right now, he said. I said, what do you mean, right now? Can't it wait? My heart started racing. He said come the way I was. The only thing I did was wash my face and clean my hands because they were dirty from peeling potatoes. Then off I went into the studio.' Though there's only about five minutes on the show, we talked for well over an hour, polishing off most of a bottle of rum while we were at it. He told me about his parents, about how he started singing in carnivals when he was eleven years old. Before we left, he sang me a song – 'Dos Gardenias' – and signed my copy of the album. 'Para mi amigo Hector', except he spelt it 'Hetor'. 'Amigos para siempre'. Cool. Especially poignant now that he's no longer with us.

THE AMAZON

AMAZONIAN VIAGRA. HOT AND SWEET. YOU POUR IT OUT AND SLAM IT BACK, LIKE TEQUILA. ABOUT AN HOUR LATER, YOU GET THIS WARM, SILKY SENSATION IN YOUR STOMACH, JUST BELOW THE BELLY BUTTON.

'It is not only for the dick,' says Moses, our guide. He's got the poshest English accent I've ever heard. Absolutely splendid, old bean. The word 'dick' sounds completely out of place. 'Not alone is it for dick,' he says, 'but for the energy of the whole area.'

'The excess,' he goes on, 'you can piss out.'

'I see, Moses,' I said. 'With your dick perhaps?'

'Yes. Your dick.'

God knows what was in the stuff. A dark, murky-coloured liquid with these long sticks like celery or rhubarb. Whatever it was, the bottle broke before we left Brazil. Soaked everything in the case.

Back home six months later, Gerry Ryan invited me on the radio. It was just after we'd won the three IFTAs for the Amazon show. Best entertainment, best lifestyle and best Irish language. Gerry was interested in the Viagra. Did I ever bring that bottle back from the jungle? Not wanting to disappoint, I decided to recreate it in Hector's kitchen. Caster sugar and Bovril, sweet chilli sauce, cumin, cinnamon sticks, herbs, two bits of muck and two rocks. Gerry didn't even flinch. Knocked it back in one, not a bother on him. Said it was great stuff altogether.

These shows wouldn't have worked half so well in English. The Amazon proved that. Celdo took over as our guide in the second half of the trip. He had taken us about six hours from any kind of civilization, way up the jungle to the Tariano, a small settlement of indigenous

people still living more or less as their ancestors had thousands of years before. They had no Irish, I spoke no Tariano, but we still managed to get together and beat out some Connemara Sean Nós.

More than any other place I had been to up to that point, the Amazon just blew me away. There was its sheer size for a start. Half the time, the river was so wide you couldn't see the other side.

The year before we arrived, they'd discovered 300 kilometres of the thing that they'd never knew existed. Three hundred kilometres lying hidden in the jungle for thousands of years. People live their whole lives on the water. There are floating petrol stations, convenience stores, restaurants, chemists, internet cafés, you name it. The first morning in Manaus, the capital of the Amazonas region, we checked out a huge meat and fish market down on the water. Nothing would put you off your breakfast quicker. Eight o'clock in the morning and packed. Besides every kind of swimmer – from piranha to crayfish – they had these chickens that they boiled whole, then cut open to show us the half-formed eggs, ready cooked inside. Gross.

We left by speedboat from Manaus, and the further we got from the city, the more beautiful the scenery. The water kept changing colour, from pink to aquamarine to green. We saw alligators sliding in from the mud banks, dolphins churning in the water. As we approached our destination, the boat veered off into successively smaller and calmer tributaries before eventually coming out into this vast, sunken landscape, as if millions of

acres of fields had been flooded. Progress slowed right down. We meandered left and right, negotiating overhanging trees and weird-looking vegetation rising up out of little islands in the water.

As Celdo brought the boat into the shore, we could see them all lined up outside their big communal hut, dressed to the nines in all the ceremonial gear. It was like something out of *National Geographic* – I half expected to hear The Mission music come blaring out from the trees. Feather headdresses, huge racks of beads, short little tunics and grass skirts. They had hand drums and pan pipes and as soon as they saw our boat, the band struck up. But the little kids. When they saw me coming through the trees they freaked out and ran in behind their ma's and da's bare brown legs. Coming up the river on the speedboat the previous day, I'd been a bit lax with the sun cream and got the worst facial sunburn I ever got. Underneath the red hair, I'd a big red beetroot of a head with the two panda eyes from the sunglasses.

After the concert, Celdo brought me round and introduced me to the grandfather, the grandmother and the many sons. It was all gestures and smiles and big, happy, nodding heads. Once upon a time, they all lived by hunting and nothing else. They had blowpipes and these short little arrows, fletched with feathers and tipped with poison. I still have the one they gave me, and it still works.

They carried out a table set with a few crude wooden bowls and a big black preserved

WE LEFT BY SPEEDBOAT FROM MANAUS, AND THE FURTHER WE GOT FROM THE CITY, **THE MORE BEAUTIFUL THE SCENERY. THE WATER KEPT CHANGING COLOUR, FROM PINK TO AQUAMARINE TO GREEN. WE SAW ALLIGATORS SLIDING IN FROM THE MUD BANKS, DOLPHINS CHURNING IN THE WATER.** AS WE APPROACHED OUR DESTINATION, THE BOAT VEERED OFF INTO SUCCESSIVELY SMALLER AND CALMER TRIBUTARIES BEFORE EVENTUALLY COMING OUT INTO THIS VAST, SUNKEN LANDSCAPE

> **THEY ALL LIVED BY HUNTING AND NOTHING ELSE.** THEY HAD BLOWPIPES AND THESE SHORT LITTLE ARROWS, FLETCHED WITH FEATHERS AND TIPPED WITH POISON. I STILL HAVE THE ONE THEY GAVE ME, AND IT STILL WORKS.

alligator head. They were probably expecting more of a reaction, but after locusts in Beijing and snails in France, there's not much that I'd be nervous of eating any more. I tore a hunk of flesh off the snout and scraped it through the little bowl of raw salt. Not bad. A tangy, fishy flavour. Chewy, like tuna steak. To wash it down, they had this high-strength jungle juice, which tasted just like Linden Village with about ten spoons of sugar through it. Like anywhere else on the planet, once the boys had a few scoops in them, the singing started up again. They had these long, decorated poles which they beat on the ground to keep time. The rhythms weren't a thousand miles from Sean Nós, and, since conversation wasn't an option, I just starting singing.

Sí do mhaimo í, sí do mhaimo í
Sí do mhaimo í, sí cailleach an airgid
Sí do mhaimo í, ó Bhaile Iorrais Mhór í
Is gcuireadh sí í gcoistí ar bhóithre Chois Fharraige

A real old Connemara song. Without any planning, any forethought, the whole thing just came together brilliantly. These lads in all the native gear beating time to a song from another ancient culture. It was one of those wonderful moments that just happen, and one that all three of us are still really proud of.

No matter where you are in the world, between five and seven in the evening, the mosquitoes get busy. They pack their little bags, climb into their little helicopters and come looking for succulent white flesh. So you have to be prepared. Besides the malaria pills you start taking three weeks before you leave home, there's all the anti-mosquito chemicals. Stuff you wash your clothes in, stuff you wash your hair in. Long sleeves and long trousers are essential, as are the cans of insect repellent.

The good thing about travelling with Evan, though, is that they all tend to go for his juicy Mountbellew calves, and he's never half as careful about covering up as myself and Rosco. As soon as I heard them coming, I took out the spray and doused myself. The tribe thought this was gas. Silly, red-faced Irishman with his bug spray. But I got the can and started spraying them all. Gave the chief a little squirt up his skirt. They thought this was even funnier. Proof, if it were needed, that arse humour is universal.

This close to the Equator, night falls in minutes. By the end of the stay, Rosco's batteries had run out, and we had to do the closing sequence by the light of a couple of torches. We didn't leave it a moment too soon. Just as we were climbing back into the boat, we could hear a big pleasure craft chugging up the river. This shrill American voice. 'Harry! Harry! Look at all this mud! How are we going to get off, Harry?' Out they poured, about forty tourists, fat and unsteady in these beekeeper hats. Talk about breaking the spell. I turned round to Rosco and said, thanks be to Jaysus they didn't arrive on camera before this, they'd have totally ruined it.

But a day later, I spot one of the chief's sons in our hotel. In feathers and beads? Me arse. Standing in the foyer in all this khaki gear, talking on a mobile phone and smoking a fag. Well for feck's sake. I call the boys down. Look at this. Been a lot of progress among the primitive indigenous peoples of the Brazilian rainforest in the last twenty-four hours, hasn't there? That night we decided that the whole thing was a bit of a con. We imagined the lot of them lounging in a hidden condominium in the trees, watching Sky Sports and jabbering on walkie-talkies. 'Yeah, who's coming down? An Irish crew? Right! Do a bit of dancing? Got you, right . . . OK people, feathers! Beads! Five minutes to curtain!'

There's something weird and scary about climbing into a canoe in the dead of night. The river was pitch black, there were lightning storms crackling off in the distance as Moses and his assistant, Crocodile Dundee, led us away from the hotel and up through the water. We kept straight ahead for half an hour, before Moses, at the helm, steered us off through the trees. Back again into this huge, flooded landscape. A vast lake clogged up with trees and vegetation, the water alive with things squirming and splashing, huge, nightmarish insects dive-bombing Rosco's lens. Here we slowed down and Crocodile hunkered down at the top of the boat, shining his torch out into the water. We were looking for caiman, the South American alligators that we'd seen sliding off the mud into the water earlier in the day. It's maybe twenty minutes before Moses nudges me and points it out. A little orange jewel shining above the surface of the water about thirty yards from the boat. We strike out towards it, but it disappears into the water before we get there. Then again. Another little orange point of light reflected in Crocodile's torch, but, like the first time, it drops down into the river as soon as we get close.

It's just like lamping rabbits. The light is so bright, it's supposed to blind the caiman, and he's held stock still until we get there. That's the theory anyway. But after an hour, all we've got is one scared little bird.

Then the insects realize there's all this tender white flesh in the neighbourhood and they get busy. Something evil gets up my shirt, and while I'm dancing around trying to get rid of the nasty little bastard, Evan - who hates boats - is clinging to the sides, going 'Don't Shake The Boat! Don't Shake The Boat!' Crocodile cops on that our camera light is causing the problem. It's casting our shadow on the water so that the caiman can see us coming. Off goes the light, and within minutes, Crocodile is hunched down at the edge of the boat about to swoop on this little two-foot alligator sitting on the edge of the water minding his own business.

We wrapped things up at eleven o'clock at night in the middle of the Amazon with me holding this little caiman doing the final piece to camera. I passed him across to Moses. To finish off the show, I said, Moses is going to put this little lad to sleep. As Moses stretched him out on the edge of the boat, my mother, at home in Navan, grabbed the remote and turned the thing off. Whatever way I had said it, whatever way Moses was stretching out the little fella, she thought that he was about to draw back, do a big Karate chop and off with his head.

But he survived. We popped him back over the side, and off he swam, none the worse for his TG4 debut.

10 BEST PLACES TO VISIT

>>> Amazonas, Brazil

Nothing you ever see on TV will ever do the Amazon justice. Just go.

>>> San Jose, Costa Rica

Chilled rural backwater. Probably the friendliest place in South America. There's loads of ecological rainforest stuff to do if you're into that. Otherwise, it's a great place to just lay back and get stuck into the Imperial beers.

>>> Ho Chi Min City, Vietnam

If Singapore is the Milton Keynes of Asia, Ho Chi Min is the Galway, and every week is race week. It's packed, it's loud, it never stops to take a breath. Or a bath.

>>> Havana, Cuba

Who says communism is no crack? Anywhere you get to sit in the sun drinking rum with Ibrahim Ferrer has to be pretty damn special.

>>> Amsterdam

In Amsterdam, if it's fun, then it's probably legal.

>>> Nashville, USA

Imagine a place where you can walk down the street wearing Wranglers, a Stetson and a pair of cowboy boots without fear of being laughed at. It's friendly, the music's great and not all rednecks are evil.

>>> Bilbao, Spain

Went for three weeks and stayed for four years. Just like home only warmer.

>>> Tokyo, Japan

Crazy neon futureland. Love hotels, capsule hotels, vending machines for everything from eggs to schoolgirls' used underpants.

>>> San Francisco, USA

The coolest city in America. The bridge, the wharf, Haight Ashbury, the carwashes. And Metallica live up in the hills.

>>> Navan

Centre of the known universe. The Boyne, the Blackwater, the new shopping centre. Brosnan, Tiernan, and Locky's Pub!

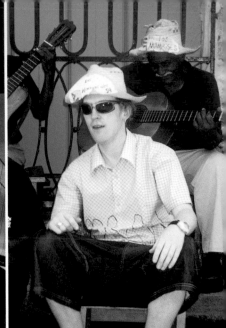

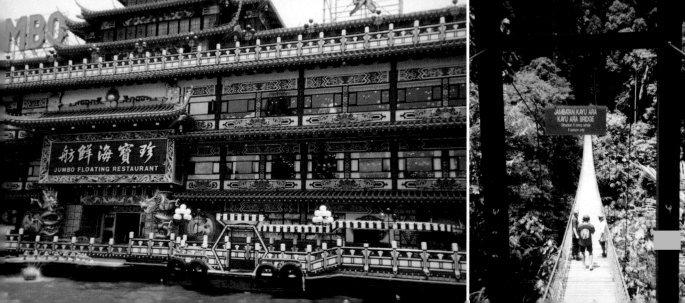

JAMAICA

GREG, OUR DRIVER, WAS THE FIRST RASTA WE MET. SIX FOOT FIVE WITH DREADS DOWN TO HIS ARSE, HE SAT HUNCHED OVER THE WHEEL OF THE VAN IN THE AIRPORT CAR PARK, HUMMING QUIETLY TO HIMSELF. As we pulled out on to the road, I saw him slot a tape into the stereo. What are we going to get now, I wondered, imagining something seriously hardcore. Bit of dub reggae? King Tubby? Lee Perry? Some new dancehall hybrid maybe?

None of the above. Michael Jackson. Instead of monstrous bass sounds we got this squeaky version of 'Beat It'. I leaned in to the front. Excuse me, Greg. 'Yah, Mon.' Any chance of some local sounds? Slow shake of the head, big, wide grin. 'No, mon, no reggae. Michael Jackson! Da king of pop.'

Da Bob Marley Foundation wanted $1,000 to allow us to film inside the museum. A thousand bucks for a few photos, a few gold discs and a couple of stage outfits? Not worth it. But we handed over a few quid to get an interview with Sharon, his daughter. This girl came sauntering down the steps of the house, and you knew straight away she was a Marley. Huge hat, big shades, fluorescent, multicoloured top, that cool that her da used to exude. Rosco started the camera rolling, and I went up to her. Hi, how are you doing? Sharon . . . Sharon Marney, Marvey . . . shiiiit! . . . Turned back to Evan, what's this one's surname again? Marley, says Evan, rolling the eyes . . . Sharon looks sideways at us with this big grin. 'You're havin' me on, aren't you?'

It broke the ice, got rid of the bad taste left by the demand for a grand. 'Link arms with me, Hector,' she says. 'Walk with me.' She was fifteen when her father died and by the sounds of things she never really knew him. He toured constantly. There for two weeks, gone for six months. Just before he died – of cancer in 1981 – she spoke to him over the phone from school in Canada. 'I remember our conversation clearly,' she says.

'I love you . . . Yeah, I love you too. That was our last conversation. But it was good that that was said because that wasn't said often . . . When Bob was here, he was always playing ball or getting ready to record a song or rehearsing. Bonding time was not always more than three minutes or when he comes home in the night if he falls asleep on the same pillow with you.

So for me to have had the opportunity to say "I love you" to him and him to say "I love you" too me was probably the only time I can remember that happening.'

We got another view of Marley when we met Ras Astor Black, president of the Jamaica Alliance Party down in Montego Bay. Also founder of the Rastafari Village, also chairman of the board of the proposed Bob Marley School for the Arts Institute. We understood that they were in the process of building a huge community park in honour of Marley, complete with a towering statue of the man overlooking the whole thing. But when we got down there, we saw no building works, no bulldozers . . . not so much as a navvy leaning on a spade. A couple of half-empty shacks on the beach with pictures of Bob on the walls. There's Ras inside one of them,

'BUT TO THESE LADS, BOB IS WAY MORE THAN A SINGER. 'A HERO, A PROPHET,' SAYS RAS. 'HE'S OUR BROTHER. IF IT WASN'T FOR HIM PUSHING THOSE POSITIVE LYRICS, THEN I PROBABLY WOULDN'T BE HERE.'

sitting with his mates round a rough wooden table. And on the table? A big fat pot full of pot. Everybody grinning broadly and talking very, very slowly...Did they even have a plan of this park they were supposed to be building? They did in their arse.

There was one ancient, gummy-mouthed Rasta to my right with wide, bloodshot eyes and a huge mass of grey dreads piled up on top of his head. He kept smiling and nodding but said nothing. Ras talked about the origins of Rastafari and how the Rastas were still discriminated against in Jamaican social and political life. He said that they needed to change the image of the Rasta as the ganga-smoking joker...Hmmmmmm. OK. Right.

But to these lads, Bob is way more than a singer. 'A hero, a prophet,' says Ras. 'He's our brother. If it wasn't for him pushing those positive lyrics, then I probably wouldn't be here.'

Before we travel, Evan always gets in touch with the local equivalent of Bord Fáilte. He tells them we're making a tourist programme and asks if they'd like to facilitate us. Some aren't bothered, but some shower us with welcome packs and guides and souped-up Hiaces to take us round. If we're staying in a Hilton or a Sheraton, it's usually because the tourist board wants to make a good impression. Jamaican Tourism wanted to make a good impression. Besides the Kingston Hilton, we got Colin the guide, an Eton-educated, beautifully spoken Jamaican of English parentage. Him and a six-foot-five Rasta who couldn't stand reggae.

Rosco and Evan, both big into their golf, started working on Colin early in the trip. Evan had read about this newly developed course set into the hills above Montego Bay. The White Witch Golf Club. Highly challenging course, stunning scenery...but very expensive and very exclusive. Every so often, Evan would say something like: 'What we'd love to do, Colin, is get a few shots for the holiday show' – when it suits him we're a holiday show – 'of Hector playing a little golf. It would be just super for golf tourism from Ireland.'

'Leave it with me,' says Colin. And fair play to him, he set it up for our last day. The only problem was finding clothes. They allowed neither shorts nor short sleeves. I had to go out and buy a shirt with a collar on it.

The manager came out to meet us as we arrived. 'So delighted to have you here! Such a wonderful opportunity to promote our club in your beautiful country.' Evan, who can ooze charm when he wants to, was all over him. 'Absolutely. We're a great golfing nation, we'll take some beautiful shots, play a round or two . . . it will be fantastic.'

Rosco didn't even put a tape in the camera.

He brought it along all right, but it sat idle in the back of the cart through all eighteen holes. Each of us was assigned an individual caddy. Mine wore a snow-white jump-suit. The minute you'd hit the ball, he'd be off down the hill like a terrier. 'Got it, sir! Found it! One hundred-and-twenty-six feet from the tee, sir! Great shot, sir!' It was embarrassing. 'Clean your ball, sir? Cold drink, sir?'

Once we finished, we met the manager back at the clubhouse. He asked if he could watch while we wrapped up the segment. So out came the tapeless camera and I had to act like I was doing a piece. I could hardly keep a straight face. Rosco there squinting into the lens, and me doing the Judith Chalmers bit. What a wonderful place the White Witch is, superb natural surroundings, beautiful course, well worth a visit . . . Then I switched to Irish. 'Ceapann an fear sin go bhfuil mise ag caint faoin golf ach níl tuairim dá laghad aige nach bhfuil aon tape istigh sa cheamara.'

'ROSCO THERE SQUINTING INTO THE LENS, AND ME DOING THE JUDITH CHALMERS BIT. WHAT A WONDERFUL PLACE THE WHITE WITCH IS, SUPERB NATURAL SURROUNDINGS, BEAUTIFUL COURSE, WELL WORTH A VISIT...THEN I SWITCHED TO IRISH. **'CEAPANN AN FEAR SIN GO BHFUIL MISE AG CAINT FAOIN GOLF ACH NÍL TUAIRIM DÁ LAGHAD AIGE NACH BHFUIL AON TAPE ISTIGH SA CEAMARA.'**

> **WHEN THE TOURISTS COME TO JAMAICA, THEY COME TO KINGSTON ON THE SOUTH COAST OR MONTEGO BAY ON THE NORTH. INLAND, YOU'LL NEVER SEE A WHITE FACE. THEY CALL IT COCKPIT COUNTRY BECAUSE IT'S UP AND DOWN, UP AND DOWN; ENDLESS HILLS AND VALLEYS LAID OUT IN THE SAME REPEATING PATTERN.**

When the tourists come to Jamaica, they come to Kingston on the south coast or Montego Bay on the north. Inland, you'll never see a white face. They call it cockpit country because it's up and down, up and down; endless hills and valleys laid out in the same repeating pattern. We stopped to get some panoramic shots of the scenery and a bite to eat in a little roadside stall on the way to Montego from Kingston. Down the way, a primary school was breaking up for the afternoon. As soon as the kids saw the white guys and the camera, they came running up to check us out. Little blue uniforms like an English prep school. You can see that English influence everywhere – the country is only independent forty years. They were there, 'Hello, hello, how are you, what are you doing?' I'm out in the middle of the group chatting away, like I've done hundreds of times before.

Then I took off the shades. All these little smiles froze. One little girl burst into tears. Another started screaming. Jesus Christ, Jesus Christ, what is it? Panic rippled through them and, as one, they turned and ran. Off back towards the school like they were being chased by a panther. 'It's your eyes,' says Colin, the guide. 'They've never seen blue eyes before.'

The second we climbed out of the car in Montego Bay, the three boys were on top of us. 'Hello, my friend! Welcome to Montego Bay. Respect, Jah, one love, Rastafari! Come, my friend, we show you around.'

You'll find lads like this in every town in the world. Hanging around outside the pool hall, one-third wino, one-third ex-druggie, one-third lunatic. Always slightly criminal. If you're looking for Rasta, they can be Rasta. Always on the look-out for a quick buck, scared stiff of work but could talk the hind legs off a donkey. They saw the three white boys and the camera, and it was feeding time at the zoo. Feck it, we said, sure we'll give them a chance. And they were gas. The self-appointed head gombeen got very annoyed any time either of the other two tried to get his spake in, any time his position was threatened.

'Now, my friend, here we are in da centre of town.'

'What are you talking about, dis isn't da centre of town, fool.'

'Who is doing da talking here?'

'You don't know what you are talking about.'

'You shut your mouth, you won't tell him, I will tell him, fool.'

And so on. In the end, there was just no getting rid of them, so I just did a runner. When they got back to the car with Evan and Rosco, Evan paid them off with a few Red Stripe beers. 'Is dis all we get?' They were indignant. 'We are professional tour guides!'

RIO

OUR DAY OFF IN THE AMAZON. THE THREE OF US WERE SITTING ON THE BALCONY OF THE ARIAU TOWERS, FISHING FOR PIRANHA. Of all the hotels we had been in, this was one of the best. An amazing wooden structure built at tree-top level at the meeting of the Rio Negro and Ariau Creek, bang in the middle of the jungle. Four miles of walkways and a honeymoon suite 110 feet above the water hollowed out of a mahogany tree. Monkeys, macaws and parrots all over the place. They told us that Bill Gates and his family had been here the week before on his laethanta saoire.

We were tossing lumps of meat over the side, watching the fishies going mad for it down below. Ice bucket full of beer in the corner. Nice.

It was the halfway point in the South American trip. We had a holiday coming up in about a week's time. All three girlfriends were flying out from Dublin to meet us in Rio. Unbeknownst to the boys – or anyone else – I had something special planned.

'Lads,' I said. 'You know the way we've ten days off when the girls arrive? Well, next Tuesday, myself and Dympna are getting married, and ye're the best men.'

It was an emotional moment. I couldn't look at the two boys. Rosco's going, 'I don't believe it, how the fuck did you keep that one to yourself?'

That was pretty much the stag party.

About eight months earlier, we were lying in bed one night, and I said to Dympna, 'If I can get a priest, right, do you want to get married in Rio?' She was there, 'Don't be stupid. Married? Rio? Turn off that light . . . ' But over the next few weeks, when she saw I was serious, she came round to the idea. We said we'd do it, and tell no one but the two mammies.

Finding the priest was way easier than I expected. After a bit of to-ing and fro-ing, the consulate gave me a list of names and numbers. At the top, Fr John Cribben.

From Shanagolden in County Limerick, he had been forty years in Brazil and now divided his time between a parish in a poor part of Rio and a military barracks where he served as chaplain. I called him up and explained what I wanted to do. He listened quietly for a few minutes, then, when I stopped talking, he says, 'Tell me this.'

Yeah?

'How's the hurling going over there?'

After the hurling, there was the Gaelic football, the rugby and the soccer. Then the racing. It wasn't 'til he was fully briefed on current sporting events in Ireland that he got round to the reason I'd called in the first place. He took me through the stuff we'd need to arrange at home. 'Make sure you've all your papers,' he says, 'and I'll marry you, no bother.'

We flew into Rio on a high and, with the promise of a ten-day holiday once we'd finished, we got stuck into filming right away. Evan had set up an interview with Jorge Guinle, a genuine, honest-to-Jaysus playboy. Back in the forties and fifties his family owned half of Rio, and smooth-talking Jorge used to fly in half of Hollywood to party the night away in the Guinle family's Copacabana Palace Hotel. Charlie Chaplin and John Wayne were regular visitors. He once shared a flat with Errol Flynn. Get this, though: over two decades, he seduced the following: Marilyn Monroe, Rita Hayworth, Veronica Lake, Lana Turner, Jane Russell, Anita Ekberg and Jayne Mansfield. The day we met him, 86-year-old Jorge had a drop-dead gorgeous 23-year-old – a good six inches taller than him – hanging on his arm. When I asked him about the crack that used to go on, he started talking about the war years. 'You didn't know if you were going to die the next day. Everyone was fucking everyone else.'

He died about eighteen months later. Fr Cribben called me up and sent over a clipping from a newspaper. We weren't aware of it at the time, but the cash had run out by the time I met him, and Jorge died more or less broke. Money or no money, he was still a regular at high-society parties right up to his final illness. At eighty-eight years of age, he was still making the gossip columns.

Rio was a dodgy spot at night. During the day too, if you weren't careful. We took a tour through the Favelas, this maze of narrow cobbled streets up on the hills where upwards of a third of the city's population lives. Though they're basically a big squatter settlement, this isn't corrugated iron and plywood, this isn't shanty-town. You've pubs, shops and houses built into the side of the hill. Here's where the people who run Rio live: the waiters, the cooks, the cleaners, the shop people. They may not be the elite, but everyone has the most incredible panoramic views, and though the place has a bad name, we ran into more trouble down in the posh part of town later that night. We had the camera out and were trying to knock a bit of crack out of the locals. This young lad was coming against me, I said, hello, shook hands with him. Big broad grin. 'Hola, hola, hola, OK, OK. Todo bene, OK, OK.' He reaches round the other hand, tries to undo the clip on the watchstrap. The neck on him. As soon as I pulled my arm away, he ran off. I chased him a few yards and shouted after him in Spanish, I'll douse you in sheep-dip, you little Brazilian bollix.

The night before the girls were due to arrive, I got word that Oireachtas na Gaeilge had awarded me Irish-speaking Personality of the Year, and I had to record an acceptance speech and courier it back in time for the ceremony in Clontarf. Apart from a lawnmower in a Christian Brothers' draw about twenty years ago, I'd never won anything in my life, so it was a real thrill to be singled out like that. Evan, fair play to him, managed to bag us a great hotel in Rio, a five-star on Copacabana beach, and that night we had great fun doing the Sorry-I-Can't-Be-With-You thing. Up on the hotel's rooftop garden in a Hawaiian shirt. Hello from Rio, where it's a balmy twenty-six degrees at nine o'clock in the evening. Sin trá Copacabana taobh thiar dom. Míle buíochas do gach duine as ucht an vótáil, míle buíochas do mo clann agus do mo cairde. Tá súil agam go bhfuil sé ag stealladh báistí anocht i mBaile Átha Cliath ... Then in comes this tray with an enormous strawberry daiquiri. Sláinte. Go raibh míle maith agaibh arís. Cheesy as bejaysus, but fun.

I DIDN'T EVEN GO OUT TO SEE THE CHURCH.
NO FLOWERS, NO FLOWER-GIRLS, NO DECORATIONS,
NO CORKAGE, NO CAKE, NO BEEF OR SALMON,
NO BAND, NO WALTZING AUNTIES, NO DISCO
AFTERWARDS. NO ROWS. NO FUSS AT ALL.

I had called Fr Cribben from Costa Rica to make sure we were on track. Because I'd been away from home for a couple of months at this stage, I couldn't give him anything on the Munster championship, so it was a short conversation. 'I'll see you in a couple of weeks,' he said. 'We're all set.'

On the flight from Dublin, Dympna kept the news under wraps until they were halfway over, then told the two girls that they'd be the bridesmaids at our wedding.

I didn't even go out to see the church. No flowers, no flower-girls, no decorations, no corkage, no cake, no beef or salmon, no band, no waltzing aunties, no disco afterwards. No rows. No fuss at all. All six of us piled into the van on the Tuesday morning and our driver, Louis, took us out to Fr Cribben's parish. The girls had got the hair and nails done the night before. Evan, who's a great singer, was going to give us his rendition of 'She Moves Through The Fair'. Rachel and Caroline would do a reading each. When we got out to the church, this small little church in a rundown suburb, there was bunting strung up across the door. Not for us, just left over from a festival the day before. Fr Cribben was waiting in the parochial house next door. He had little tricolours up on the wall alongside a picture of the Pope. A little patch of Limerick a couple of thousand miles from home.

Inside the chapel – as simple as they come – there was a woman practising the organ. I went up to her and asked if she'd stay on and play during the ceremony. 'Sure,' she said, 'I'd love to.' Now, besides Evan, we had this beautiful Portuguese singing. Fr Cribben was great. 'This is the first time in my forty-two years as a priest,' he said, 'where I know all my congregation and can welcome them here by name.'

He told us where to go for the honeymoon too. Buzios. About two hours north of Rio, a fishing village sitting at the end of a long peninsula. We stayed in a quiet little guesthouse that had a swimming pool overlooking the ocean. One of the most beautiful places I've ever been. On the trip down, we drank about fifty Brazilian beers, singing every mile of the way.

'Jaysus,' says Rosco at one point. 'Pull over here, pull over.' A roadside pharmacy.

'What is it, what are we stopping here for?'

'Viagra.'

'Hah?'

'No, no, not for me, it's for me oul fella's 60th birthday.'

You don't need a prescription over there, and it's a fraction of the price.

Must have seemed a bit odd to the girl behind the counter. The three girls dressed up to the nines out in the van, the three boys off their heads in the shop, trying to explain that they needed as much Viagra as they could carry.

'ONE BY ONE WE FELL. I WAS THE FIRST TO NOTICE IT. **THAT WINDY, GURGLY STOMACH. SPLUTTERY FARTS THAT'D HAVE YOU NERVOUSLY FLEXING THE CHEEKS TO SEE IF THEY WERE LIQUID OR NOT.** THEN BANG. JACKS, JACKS, GOTTA HAVE A JACKS. OH THE RELIEF. COMPLETELY CLEANED MYSELF OUT IN ABOUT FOUR HOURS.'

NA RITHÍ

IN ALL THE PLACES WE'VE BEEN AND ALL THE DODGY UNIDENTIFIABLE STUFF I'VE EATEN ON THE SIDE OF THE ROAD, I WAS ONLY LAID LOW TWICE. HERE'S A NEW WORD FOR THE CLASS: BUINNEACH. REPEAT IT TO YOURSELF. BUINNEACH. A WORD THAT TRICKLES GENTLY DOWN THE BACK OF THE LEG.

The first time in China. Out at the Great Wall one morning, there was nowhere to eat but one of these rip-off fast food places. We all had the same thing. Burgers. One by one we fell. I was the first to notice it. That windy, gurgly stomach. Spluttery farts that'd have you nervously flexing the cheeks to see if they were liquid or not. Then bang. Jacks, jacks, gotta have a jacks. Oh the relief. Completely cleaned myself out in about four hours.

As it turned out I was lucky. Poor oul Rosco spent the bones of three days perched on the edge of the bowl. He thought he was going to die. We arrived in Seoul on the third day and I went round to the chemist, explained his predicament as best I could to the little guy behind the counter. Whatever bottle he gave me corked Rosco anyway and we were able to get a bit of work done. But that first night, in Beijing, we were in this restaurant. Rosco of course wasn't eating but myself and Evan felt we were ready to try something again. I still couldn't stray too far from the jacks though. Halfway through the meal, the need came on me. There was only one toilet. And that toilet was one of those Asian jobs. Where we westerners like to sit, Asians prefer to squat, so all they get is this hole in the ground. I don't know how they do it. After about thirty seconds on your hunkers, your thighs start to ache, your knees start to wobble and you have to try and balance yourself against the wall. Anyway, this time I got the stance 100% wrong, and before I knew what I was at, I'd only gone and sprayed the back wall. Ah shite. Bang on

cue, the door starts rattling. 'Excuse please! You finish?' Ah…hang on a sec, hang on. Asians don't go in for toilet paper either. All I had to deal with the mess was a thin little j-cloth type thing and a bottle of disinfectant. I was there with the fobhristí around the ankles, still not sure if there wasn't more to come, hooshing water from the sink against the wall, trying to undo the damage.

And the smell. There's no smell quite like Irish buinneach. Caustic. Reminiscent of snack-boxes and Harp. I knew the second I opened the door that that smell would waft out, Bisto-like, to fill the entire restaurant, and there'd be no mistaking who owned it.

Half an hour later, I unlocked the door and made straight for the table, past the queue of about five lads hovering outside. C'mon c'mon, I said to the two boys, throwing a few quid on the table, let's get out of here.

But the worst ever was in Lima, the day of Ireland's opening game against Cameroon in the 2002 World Cup. Never found out where I picked the thing up. The two boys got up at four a.m. to go and look at the match, but I had to lie curled up in the bed. The slightest movement and the gut would demand a return to the toilet. Three days, all I did was go back and forth between bathroom and bed, picking up the phone only to order more jacks paper from reception. I lambasted the toilet, left it with cracks running up the side. Starts out as sweetcorn-like debris, until any remnants of anything you've ever eaten are gone. Then it's entirely liquid. Dirty water like you'd see in a puddle on a building site. But by day three, it was still coming, this time as pure and clear as a mountain spring.

HECTOR'S GUIDE TO HEALTHCARE ON THE ROAD

>>> Insect repellents

- *Repel, packed full of DEET.* **They hate that stuff.**

>>> Creams

teatree

CALAMINE

- *Tea tree oil cream* **for burns**
- *Savlon antiseptic cream* **for cuts and scrapes to elbows and knees**
- *Zovirax* **for cold sores**
- *Calamine lotion* **if sun screen fails**
- *Bonjela* **for the mouth ulcers**
- *Rinstead* **if mouth ulcers are more persistent**
- *Moisturiser and Vitamin E Cream* **to keep skin beautiful and young looking**

Bonjela

Rinstead

Vit E

>>> Pills

- *Doxycycline* **for Malaria**
- *Solpadeine* **– six pounds of, for hangovers**
- *Imodium* **or** *Arete* **to cork the flow when the trots strike**
- *Motilium* **to calm the belly after dodgy food bought on side of road**
- *Paracetamol* **Paracetamol for sundry aches and pains**

>>> Herbal Oils for Soothing Bath to Ease Away Aches & Pains after Stressful Day Arsing around in the Sun

- *Bergamot*
- *Juniper*
- *Vetiver*

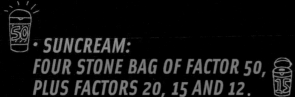

- **SUNCREAM:**
FOUR STONE BAG OF FACTOR 50,
PLUS FACTORS 20, 15 AND 12.

>>> **Shots**

- *Tetanus*
- *Cholera*
- *Diphtheria*
- *Hepatitis A*
- *Hepatitis B*
- *Rabies* **(to protect against evil monkeys)**

>>> **Also**

- *Huge roll of sticking plasters*
- *42 cans of Lynx Afrika deodorant*

SUDOCREM – MONSTER POT.
INSERT THREE LARGE FINGERS
AND SPREAD LIBERALLY ON
GUSSET AREA FOLLOWING
SWEAT RASH OUTBREAK

A CAUTIONARY TALE

IT WAS A TINY LITTLE SPOT. Didn't even have a yellow head. A tiny inoffensive little spot that wouldn't have caused anyone any bother, that should have been left alone. But it's a ten-hour flight from London to Mumbai. You've seen the in-flight movies, there's nothing to read, the two boys are dozing, no one else speaks English. You're bored out of your mind. You get up, you walk around, you go to the bathroom, you wash your hands, you fuss around with your hair, you wash your hands again. Check the watch. Two minutes have passed. Eventually, you're going to start picking at things. It's only a matter of time.

He's a stubborn little bastard and it takes about ten minutes of squeezing and scratching before I get him to pop. Wash the face and hands again, back to the seat. I think no more about it.

The hotel in Mumbai turns out to be pretty dodgy. The beds are damp and there's this sodden mess of carpet in the hall. We check out after one night, but before we do, I wake up to a spot that's quadrupled in size. It's after upgrading itself to a hive, and has this dark red core area bang in the centre. What do I do? I go at the little fucker again, that's what I do. And of course next day, the day we're supposed to start filming, it is now a full grown, unadulterated, don't-fuck-with-me boil, about the same size and shape as the Hill of Tara.

Ah shite.

I had to do the whole of the Bollywood Show with this yoke on the left-hand side of my face. When we got to England to meet the Red Arrows the following week, I called my mother from the Holiday Inn in Lincoln. Mam, I said, what am I going to do about this thing? Bathe it, she said. Get the TCP, get the cotton wool, get a kettle of boiling water. Bathe it, bathe it, bathe it. I did exactly as she said, and after about an hour and a half, it burst. It was like something out of a horror movie. This volcano of rich green pus that just kept coming and coming and coming. It was hypnotic, it was like trying to drag yourself away from the scene of a car crash. Forty minutes, it poured fourth the vilest-looking shite you ever saw.

The moral of the story boys? Don't pick it. And if you have to, don't do it in the dirty recycled air of a jumbo jet on the way to Mumbai. Have a little tug instead.

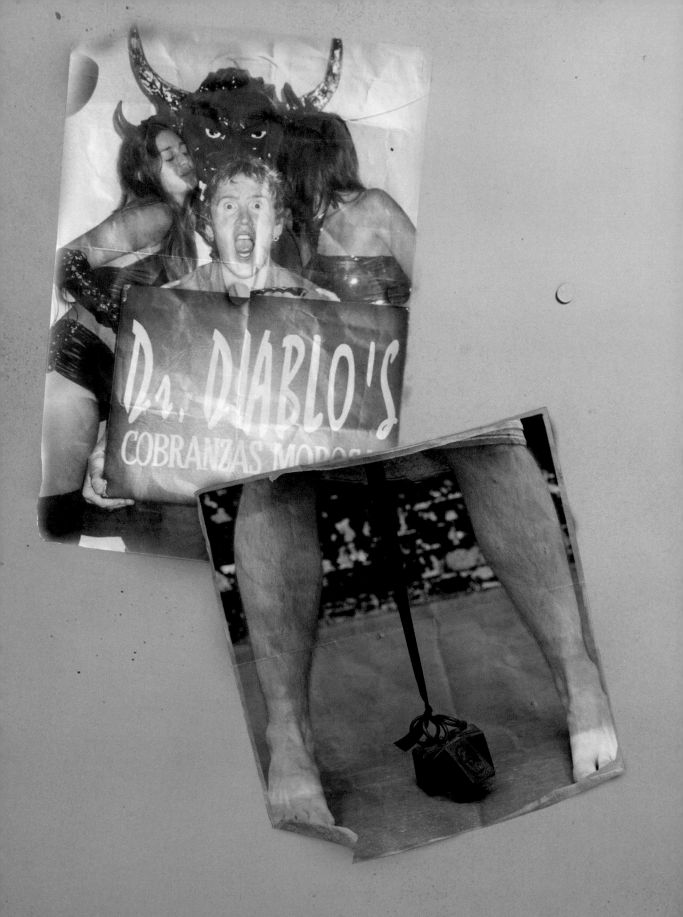

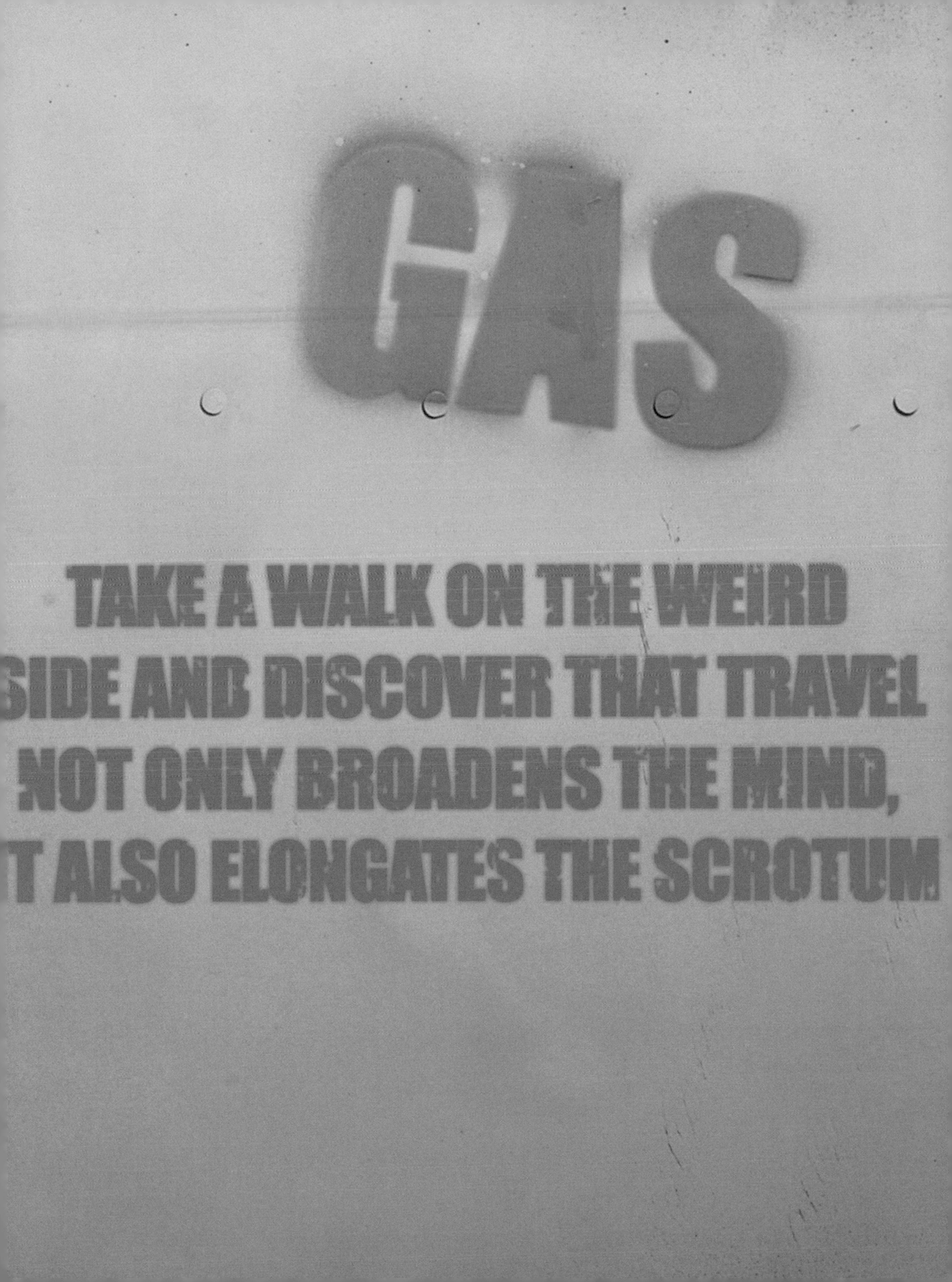

GAS

TAKE A WALK ON THE WEIRD
SIDE AND DISCOVER THAT TRAVEL
NOT ONLY BROADENS THE MIND,
IT ALSO ELONGATES THE SCROTUM

ENGLAND

EVERY TIME URI GELLER LOOKS DIRECTLY INTO THE CAMERA, JUSTIN THE CAMERAMAN GETS THIS WAIL OF STATIC AND HAS TO PULL OFF THE HEADPHONES SO'S HE WON'T BURST AN EARDRUM.

Uri keeps looking at the camera.

He's got this stare, this hypnotic 1,000-yard stare, that nails you to the couch. Maybe he always looks like this, maybe it's because we're half an hour late. We tell him about Justin and the static, and he starts to get all excited. 'Ah, wait a minute!' He holds up the finger. 'Maybe it's paranormal!'

We look at each other and shrug. Why not? It's the paranormal that has us here in the first place. We're on the final leg of our journey into the murky world of ghosts, witches, psychics, the occult and the various characters that get into this sort of thing. I'm here to get me spoons bent, which, by the looks of things, is a profitable business. Uri's London retreat isn't exactly modest. Gleaming Rolls Royce cooling on the gravel, vast, palatial house set among pristine gardens sweeping gently to the banks of the Thames. Inside isn't half as kooky as you'd expect for a psychic. All this abstract sculpture – he studied art under Salvador Dali – alongside framed photos of Uri with his high-profile mates – Michael Jackson in one, George Bush in another. Through the window, I catch sight of this huge glass pyramid out on the back lawn. He takes me through the ground floor, telling me that the house was built on an ancient 'healing centre'. In his large, untidy office, the phones never stop ringing. There are banks of computer screens set out on desks. 'I get about 300 emails a day,' he says. 'I answer them all...People want advice all the time. What I do is I answer them by hand, then send them to India, to Mumbai. In Mumbai, there are two young brothers who actually sit there, read my answers, type them in and email them out.'

He killed a man. Serving in the Israeli army during the Six Day War. This guy popped up from behind a rock, and it was him or Uri. 'That Jordanian is in my soul now,' he tells me.

I want to cut to the chase. Test the goods. In the arse pocket, I've a drawing of a John Deere 7920 – that's the tractor equivalent of a BMW seven series. This is Uri's other trick. Besides destroying the cutlery, he'll guess the picture. He averts the laser-beam eyes, you draw your little doodle, then he'll sit down and draw the same thing, having extracted the image from your mind using his psychic powers. He did it a few years back on the Late Late, and wowed everyone with a near-perfect replica of Gay's drawing of a house with a tree beside it.

'I close my eyes,' he says, 'and what I visualize in order to get the picture is an imaginary TV screen that I can see inside my head now.' He closes the eyes, tells me to concentrate on the picture, then cranks the intensity up a notch. 'Don't look anywhere, just stare at me!' And he gets scribbling. And he draws a tractor.

Now. I'm totally bowled over by this. I believe. Uri, I'm thinking, is the real deal. But Rosco. Rosco did all the camera work for South America and Asia. He's not here for this series, but when, over pints in The Goat a couple of weeks later, I tell him about Uri, he's there, Hector, you dope. You stupid, dopey eejit. Duped. Conned. Hoodwinked. Made an idiot of on your own TV show. You poor, stupid, bloody eejit. See, Rosco, in the meantime, has been working on this magician's TV show. He's had to sign a non-disclosure agreement, promising not to tell anyone how these seemingly amazing tricks were done. He's seen more smoke and mirrors in the last few months than most people see in their entire lives.

'Cameras,' he says. 'Did you not check for cameras?'

No I didn't check for cameras, why would I check for cameras?

He rolls the eyes. 'Sure there's hidden cameras everywhere, you stupid bastard. He had some laughing at you, so he did. Ha, ha, ha, he was saying. Ha, ha. Stupid Paddy, just off the boat. I'll draw the gobshite a tractor and he'll wet himself. Ha, ha, ha. Tell us, where did you do the drawing?'

Down here on my lap, I tell him, showing him how I covered over it so no one would see.

HE HOLDS IT UP, STARTS STROKING IT BACK AND FOURTH, THERE BETWEEN THE CUP AND THE HANDLE: 'THERE IT GOES!' HE SAYS, GIVING IT THE OLD SHOWBIZ PATTER. 'THERE IT GOES! THERE IT GOES! THERE IT GOES! CAN YOU SEE IT? CAN YOU SEE IT? CAN YOU SEE IT?' AND UP GOES THE HANDLE. VISIBLY. YOU CAN SEE IT GO. I'M STARING AT IT. I DON'T SEE ANY STRINGS, ANY SMOKE**,**

'Down here on his lap!' No one can do scorn like Rosco. He shakes the head. 'I suppose he gave you the pen.'

I don't know, I tell him, I don't remember.

'He doesn't remember,' says Rosco. 'Sure there could have been a camera in the pen.' He looks sideways at me, this look like I've let the entire family down. 'You're some eejit.'

This drives me nuts, and I'm looking again at the two tractors. Maybe they're not so similar. Maybe Uri's just taken a look at me and figured, this lad's gonna draw some class of a vehicle, something like a jeep or a truck . . . which is what his drawing really looks like, more than a tractor. I'm thinking, maybe I should have tried something a bit less obvious. OK, I'm no Rolf Harris, but maybe one of those black plastic wrapping bailers, or, I don't know, the Twelve Pins from Peacocks at Maam Cross or something.

So what about the spúnóg bending then? Uri takes me into the kitchen. His daughter's in there, making a sandwich. Into the drawer, out comes the spoon. He holds it up, starts stroking it back and fourth, there between the cup and the handle: 'There it goes!' he says, giving it the old showbiz patter. 'There it goes! There it goes! There it goes! Can you see it? Can you see it? Can you see it?' And up goes the handle. Visibly. You can see it go. I'm staring at it. I don't see any strings, any smoke. The spoon's not disappearing down behind his back where he can give it a sly little wrench. 'There,' he says, 'feel that.' Ice cold. Right, I say, now I'll pick the spoon, and I delve down into the drawer, get one right from the bottom. 'Iberia' it says on the handle. From the airline. And off he goes again, giving it extra ripsie just for me. This time he leaves it down on the ground and it keeps going. The thing turns completely in on itself.

Rosco isn't buying any of it, but he doesn't have any explanation either. He takes a swig of the pint and ruminates on the colossal stupidity of man.

All right, all right, so maybe Uri isn't all he cracks himself up to be. But the day before, down in London, we met Deanna Del Monte, clairvoyant to the stars.

You'd expect a clairvoyant called Deanna Del Monte to live in some vast gothic mansion, all covered in ivy at the top of a winding avenue. But no. Something like 39 Primrose Avenue. Nondescript terraced house. Couple of kids running round the sofa where we sat, her howling at them to get their homework started for Gawd's sake. On camera, she came up with some pretty decent stuff.

I'd never been on a motorbike in my life until we did the show from Thailand the previous year. I ended up in the ditch on my first attempt. 'Have you been involved in a motorbike accident in the last eighteen months?' she asks. She also had a few things to say about the awards we won for the previous series. But off camera, with the two boys, Justin the cameraman and Rónan the producer, she really got going. In the car on the way up from Heathrow on the Monday, Justin had been telling us that he met an ex of three years' standing the previous week. They had some notion of maybe getting back together, but the whole thing fell apart very quickly. After an hour they were at each other's throats. As soon as the cameras stopped rolling, Deanna turns to Justin and says, 'I know you met her last week and you thought there was something there. There is nothing there. It's been dead for a couple of years, you shouldn't have met her last week. Forget about it. Let it go. It's finished.' Justin nearly dropped the camera.

Then she turns to Rónan. 'Look,' she says, 'you're going to have children eventually but you are very close to your little sister right now. She's almost like a best friend, isn't she?' And Rónan nearly started crying, because he is really close to his sister. She goes on: 'Your first-born child will be a girl and she's going to be the image of your sister. You won't believe how much like her she's going to be.'

All three of us left the place pretty shaken up. No smoke and mirrors here, no camera tricks. Had she the car bugged? Did she get her mate Seamus in Longford to tape all our shows on TG4 just so she could use that motorbike accident? Had she someone staking out Rónan's house in Wexford just to get the lowdown on his situation? Tá an fhírinne amuigh ansin, boys!

'ALL THREE OF US LEFT THE PLACE PRETTY SHAKEN UP. NO SMOKE AND MIRRORS HERE, NO CAMERA TRICKS. HAD SHE THE CAR BUGGED? DID SHE GET HER MATE SEAMUS IN LONGFORD TO TAPE ALL OUR SHOWS ON TG4 JUST SO SHE COULD USE THAT MOTORBIKE ACCIDENT? TÁ AN FHÍRINNE AMUIGH ANSIN, BOYS!'

Poor oul Kevin, the white witch. Struggling to get his broomsticks into the boot of the Micra.

We were on our way out to the forest, so's I could be initiated into The Craft. I was trying to do a piece to camera, I was trying to act professionally, but I couldn't stop laughing. It's like when you're at school, standing up doing your bit of reading, and some lad behind you in the seat is tickling your arse. I'd never cracked up like that on telly before, but Kevin was a gas man. Another ordinary terraced house, packed floor to ceiling with pentangles, windchimes, all that crack, and about fifty black cats. Kevin in the middle of it all, slightly tubby in drawstring trousers and a greying blond pony-tail, kind of like a record company exec. 'You've been very down at some point in your life,' he tells me. 'You can go down a very deep hole sometimes, then you come back up again.' I tell him I live beside a very deep hole in Navan. Tara Mines. The largest lead and zinc mine in the world. But in fairness. Sometimes you're happy, sometimes you're sad. As analyses go, it's not exactly brilliant, is it? He has a wand held together with insulating tape, which pretty much says it all. You'd have to travel a long way to find a set-up as half-arsed as this.

Out in the forest, things slip down another gear. This guy was supposed to be the head witch in the UK. You have certain ideas about what a head witch might get up to. You think of a vast coven. Cowled figures chanting around a huge bonfire. Blood sacrifices. Thunder and lightning, obscure mantras, bubbling cauldrons, weird rites and initiation ceremonies. At the very least a little naked frolicking. But it was just me and Kevin, along with this young one who showed up at his place for a Tarot reading and then just sort of tagged along. The three of us are standing there beside this pitiable fire in these dressing-gown things, like we're queuing for the sauna. And it's not even a

forest. Just these few trees surrounded on all sides by housing estates. Kids on their way to school are looking over, wondering what the hell is going on. 'Black magic and white magic,' says Kevin. 'It's like the Force in *Star Wars*. It's neutral. You can tap into either side of it.'

His initiation ritual isn't exactly hard going. No dangling by your nipples from the sacred oak or anything like that. He tells me I have to pass three tests: look into the bonfire without my eyes going funny. OK, done. I have to kiss the priestess. The young one starts to look shifty, but I give her a quick peck on the cheek before she can run off. 'The third one is more difficult,' he says, handing me a broomstick. 'You must go at least two feet on this.' I look at him. So I just run and jump? 'Yeah, that's it,' he says.

I'm still holding out for a little naked frolicking. Kevin, however, doesn't seem keen, and the young one double-ties her dressing gown at the suggestion. Oh well, says I, unbuckling the belt. Not the first time. Probably won't be the last.

>>>CONVERSATIONS YOU SHOULD **NEVER** *Have with Your Mother #2*

>*MAM:* **WHY** DID YOU HAVE TO TAKE YOUR CLOTHES OFF?

>HECTOR: *Mam, because it was funny.*

>*MAM:* That's **NOT** funny now, that's **NOT** FUNNY.

>HECTOR: MAM, I . . .

>*MAM: Some of that other stuff you do is funny. Taking off your clothes is not funny.* You're perfectly capable of doing a show without taking your clothes off. Why did you?

>HECTOR: MAM . . .

>*MAM:* What am I going to say to the *Sister Baptist* when she's in on Friday? What am I going to tell her? You, on the television sets of the nation, FROLICKING AROUND SOME FOREST WITH A PAIR OF NYLON SOCKS ON AND NOTHING ELSE. What am I going to say to them? I have to live in this town. It's all right for you, I have to walk down the street . . .

'SO, MR SHATNER, DO YOU MISS FLYING THE ENTERPRISE?'

HE GRUNTS. HIS EYES ARE GLAZED OVER. HE'S A MILLION LIGHT YEARS AWAY.

CAPTAIN'S LOG. STARDATE 22-7: WHY DO I COME TO THESE FUCKING THINGS? WHY THE FUCK DO I PUT MYSELF THROUGH IT? FUCKING CONVENTIONS. FUCKING SCIENCE FUCKING FICTION. WHAT I COULD REALLY USE RIGHT NOW IS –

PASADENA

I DON'T THINK I'VE EVER SEEN ANYONE AS BORED AS WILLIAM SHATNER. He's slouched on a chair in front of a *Star Trek* backdrop while this photographer flits around in front of him, snapping away. In the wings, there are about seventy hardcore fans, all gazing adoringly at him. Each of them has shelled out several hundred bucks for the privilege of having a photo taken beside the great man. Kirk, however, looks like he'd rather face the massed armies of the Klingon empire than shake another hand or sign another picture. One of his handlers scurries up to him and says something like 'There's an Irish crew here to speak to you, sir, can I send them in?' One eyebrow flickers. This must mean yes, because she comes back and tells us that Mr Shatner will see us now.

One hundred and twenty seconds, that's all we've got: 120 hard-won seconds. Rónan's been fighting for Shatner time for months, from the first day we decided we'd come to the eleventh annual Grand Slam Convention here in Pasadena. Besides the countless emails back and forth, on the day, we've had to cajole and beguile half a dozen Mandys and Kyles just to get those two lousy minutes.

'So, Mr Shatner, do you miss flying the *Enterprise*?'

He grunts. His eyes are glazed over. He's a million light years away.

Captain's Log. Stardate 22-7: Why do I come to these fucking things? Why the fuck do I put myself through it? Fucking conventions. Fucking science fucking fiction. What I could really use right now is –

'Have you ever been to Ireland?'

He jumps awake, like I've stabbed him in the arse with a compass. 'Yes,' he says. 'The fishing is terrible. The salmon are gone.' He gives me this look like it's my fault, like I've all of them at home in the bath. 'You know why?... You don't know why the

salmon are gone?' Long pause. One tenth of the interview goes on dramatic silence. 'Because they changed the trees!'

'Hah?'

They changed the trees? What the fuck is he talking about? But the handler's back to usher the man on to his next appointment. I never find out what they changed the trees into.

Half an hour later, we're in the main convention hall when he makes an impromptu appearance. They're in the middle of a memorabilia auction, trying to flog an original clapperboard, when he bounds out into the middle of the stage. Bounds. Thirty minutes earlier, he looked like he was coming down with rigor mortis. Now he's lepping around like a man half his age. The second he appears, there's this surge of people up to the front, like it's a Metallica concert. Now he's riding the wave, dancing back and forth. He's charming, he's witty, he's up to ninety. 'If we get this up to $5,000, Leonard Nimoy will sign it…with his mouth!' The place goes crazy. No, crazier.

Dollars, the convention is all about the greenbacks. Everything costs something. They've several different levels of ticket from $500 for access-all-areas right down to the yellow-pack option that'll get you no more than four yards inside the door. From ten in the morning 'til six in the evening, you've rows and rows of signing tables. The A list is up near the top. People like Peter Mayhew, the seven-foot-three giant who played Chewbacca, or David Prowse, aka Darth Vader. This quiet-spoken Englishman has one of the most sought-after signatures in town.

These days, he tells me, this is pretty much all he does. 'Last week,' he says, 'I came over for a one-day show in Las Vegas. Then I had a show in Slough on Saturday night. Monday, I was in Chesterfield. Then here. Next week I've the big one on memorabilia in Birmingham.' The A-list boys are scribbling away all day, but down at the C-list tables, you've only the occasional visitor. Here you'll find Captain Wankyarse from Mission to the Underworld VI, sitting there staring into space, chewing on the back of a pen.

'FROM TEN IN THE MORNING 'TIL SIX IN THE EVENING, YOU'VE ROWS AND ROWS OF SIGNING TABLES. THE A LIST IS UP NEAR THE TOP. PEOPLE LIKE PETER MAYHEW, **THE SEVEN-FOOT-THREE GIANT WHO PLAYED CHEWBACCA,** OR DAVID PROWSE, AKA DARTH VADER. THIS QUIET-SPOKEN ENGLISHMAN HAS ONE OF THE MOST SOUGHT-AFTER SIGNATURES IN TOWN.'

It's a cash business. Signature, that's five dollars. Signed picture, that's ten. You want your photo taken with the captain? That's another ten. The note goes into the bag under the table. Or over to the wife. Nearly all of them have wives or partners sitting behind them. Knitting or playing Sudoku, wearing an 'I Love Captain Wankyarse' badge and keeping a close eye on the dollar bills. But if there's one thing everyone has in common, from the biggest names down to the smallest, they're all about as bored as Shatner.

Most of the time it's like that scene from *Star Wars* when Han Solo walks into the bar and you've all the different species milling around. It's not just inside the convention centre either. Everywhere you go, you'll see groups of Klingons, Vulcans, Romulans, Imperial Stormtroopers, Wookie, Ferengi . . . Dozens of C3POs, She-Ras and Xenas. Also loads of freestyle aliens and freaks I don't recognize. The place is loony soup.

Of all the groups, though, you've more Klingons and Stormtroopers than any other. They stay in character the whole time. You'll never see a Stormtrooper without his helmet or a Klingon without his big, mad, scaly headpiece. We're over at a shopping centre across the road to get some lunch, and the place is overrun with them. While the Klingons kind of huddle together in tight groups, the Stormtroopers go everywhere in formation. They all have walkie-talkies.

As I pull open the door of a pizza restaurant there's a gang of them coming against us. The guy at the front of the line is talking into his radio. 'Yeah, we're down in Jimmy's Pizza Place. Where are you? Over.' With the fizzy static of the radio in the background, you can hear, 'Ah, we're all up on level four in McDonald's. Why don't you come up? Over.' And out they come, tramp tramp tramp, one after the other. Across the mall, a Darth Vader comes sauntering out of a shop with a can of Sprite. The second they see him, they all stop dead and salute. 'Vader!' Of course, because there's dozens of Vaders about, this keeps happening. As they head off up to level four, you can hear them stopping every so often and shouting 'Vader!' in unison.

Another troop comes up the escalator. At the sight of the camera, one of them calls out, 'Long live the empire!' There's this group of Klingons eating tacos at a nearby stand. One of them says, 'Yeah, ours!'

We've arranged to meet a couple of weekend Klingons who're staying in the convention hotel. Grandparents Roy and Carolyn Henderson are a special education teacher and a civil engineer by day, but come Saturday, she's Okwa and he's K'tah of the House of Roshka, Chancellor of the Imperial Klingon Armada. 'I was adopted into the house of Roshka by Kodra,' says Roy. 'The Empress Kodra. She fought with Kahless, who united the empire.'

Here are two of the most ordinary-looking people you could hope to meet. Both a little short, he's bald, she's got tight grey hair. They're cheery, welcoming and easy company. If you didn't know and were asked to guess their hobbies, you'd probably say something like, I don't know, gardening and cake decorating or something. But, as they talk, both begin to transform themselves into Okwa and K'tah. Carolyn is busy arranging her white, long-haired head piece. 'No Klingon goes into battle without a panty liner on the forehead,' she says, 'but you make sure you put the sticky side on the inside of the head piece.' By the time they've finished, they look amazing. I mean they look professionally made up. I'm given a red armband to let everyone know I'm an 'honoured guest' of the Klingon empire and downstairs we hook up with a dozen other Klingons. 'What are you doing with that Earthling?' one of them asks Roy. He hasn't seen the armband. Of all of the group, this guy looks the least convincing, but only because he's holding a Pekinese in his arms. Honest to God.

One time, Carolyn tells me, they were at this convention where the special guest was Michael Dorn, the guy who plays the Klingon Worf on *Star Trek*. Roy and Carolyn together with a dozen of their Klingon friends provided an honour guard for the actor as he left the stage. Walking down between two rows of heavily made-up fans, Dorn looks the group up and down and says in this bewildered voice, 'Why do you people do this to yourselves?' Good question, Worf. Good question.

VENEZUELA

SOME THINGS COULD ONLY WORK IN SOUTH AMERICA. Imagine your local solicitor surrounding himself with scantily clad young ones and actors in Halloween costumes, then careering down the main street in convoy to embarrass the life out of some lad who owes a client money.

But there's a big tradition of using public shame to get what you want in Latin America. And with the Venezuelan economy in tatters, there's a huge problem with bad debts. Dr Diablo claims a 70 per cent success rate. Despite how cracked the set-up appears, it's no wonder the man is kept busy.

And the set-up does look cracked. He's a fully qualified solicitor, but the degree on the wall is about the only thing that's any way normal. He has his office in the basement of the Caracas Hilton decked out like a dungeon. Flames painted on the ceiling, a big Macnas devil's head in the corner. We were met at the door by the two girls. She-devils. One of them in skin-tight silver pants and boob tube, the other in thigh-high leather boots and leather hot-pants. Discreet little set of horns on the head.

If the two women look like they've just strode off the catwalk, Dr Diablo himself looks like something out of *Scarface*. He's sitting behind his desk, loading a big fuck-off Smith and Wesson. Are those real bullets? I ask him. He waves the hand dismissively. 'It's just for intimidation,' he says and tucks the gun into his belt.

The she-devil in the silver pants explains the plan. Juan Pablo Guitierez owes $100,000, and all attempts to get him to pay the debt haven't worked. His creditors have passed the file to the Doctor, who will publicly serve papers on Guitierez at his place of business – a trendy jeans shop in the middle of town. If he doesn't pay up today, they'll take his picture and publish it in a big Dr Diablo ad in one of the national dailies. Simple, but effective.

'BIG SOUPED-UP BEACH BUGGY AND A VINTAGE JEEPSTER ALL DECKED OUT **IN DR DIABLO'S TRADEMARK BLACK, SHOT THROUGH WITH** ORANGE FLAMES. STRAIGHTAWAY YOU CAN SEE HOW WELL THE CONCEPT WORKS. AS WE CLIMB INTO THE VEHICLES, EVERYBODY ON THE STREET STOPS TO GAWK.'

Outside, the convoy is set up and ready to roll. Big souped-up beach buggy and a vintage Jeepster all decked out in Dr Diablo's trademark black, shot through with orange flames. Straightaway you can see how well the concept works. As we climb into the vehicles, everybody on the street stops to gawk. And just in case there's still someone left around who hasn't noticed us, on go the sirens and the flashing lights. The boys tear through the city like they really are cops, down pedestrianized streets, through red lights, not a bother on them.

Ten minutes later, the *Rocky Horror Picture Show* arrives at Guitierez's. The place reminds me of O'Connor's jeans shop that used to be on Middle Abbey Street years ago.

Here's the business end of Dr Diablo's circus. Everybody in Caracas knows who he is, and within seconds of us pulling up at the footpath, there's a huge press of people between us and the shop. The manageress sees what's about to happen and she comes rushing out to try some damage limitation. Only the people in suits may enter the shop, she says. Dr Diablo, clutching the legal papers, pushes through. 'I don't give a shit,' he says and strides towards the door with the entourage close behind him. She darts ahead of him again, and there's a stand-off on the street. He's calling her a cheat, saying he's been here four times and still no money. She's playing a losing game here and can't get a word in edgeways. Meanwhile, half of Caracas looks on, bemused. He gets through eventually, serves the papers and takes his snapshot. I try to knock a bit of crack out of a harassed manageress. 'If yiz don't fuckin pay,' says I in a dirty Dublin accent, 'I'll be back and I'll fuckin burn yiz out of it. No one messes with the TG4 boys.'

The flight into Caracas was half empty. There was just myself, Evan and Rosco sitting in the back of the plane on our own, wondering if we'd made a terrible mistake. The airport too, a big international airport. Empty. The guide met us at the gate. 'This is going to be very dangerous, gentlemen,' he says, pulling back the door of the van. 'People are dying in the street.'

Five days before we arrived, mass demonstrations in front of the presidential palace had led to a military coup which removed Hugo Chavez from power and installed opposition leader Pedro Carmona. Carmona immediately set about pissing everyone off, dissolving the national assembly and repealing the constitution that Chavez had adopted three years earlier. More demonstrations followed, in which thirty-five people were killed, and after just forty-seven hours in power, Carmona stepped out and Chavez stepped in again. We sat in our hotel in Costa Rica, watching the whole thing play out on CNN. Protests, speeches, chaos, rioting. Gunshots. Dead bodies. Evan called the Irish embassy in Mexico – the only Irish embassy south of Texas. Well, they said, it seems to be blowing over. You'll probably be all right. As the guide drove us in through half-empty streets, you could taste the tension in the air. The military were everywhere. Pounding the streets in twos and threes, armed to the teeth. Jeeps and personnel carriers zipping up and down past the taxis and trundling lorries. A handful of shops open. It was like everyone was slowly edging open their doors after a tornado had passed through. Checking the damage. Wondering if it was safe to come back out.

The palatial bulk of Hotel El Cid sits at the top of the Avenida San Felipe overlooking the city. That night, all but three of its fifty-two rooms were empty. I got room one, Rosco got room two and Evan got room three. Tables hadn't been cleared. The outdoor swimming pool was full of leaves, and there was a thin film of dust everywhere. One man on duty. He checked us in, showed us to our rooms and later on made us a couple of dodgy sandwiches and opened the bar. On the TV, the channels kept showing the same footage of the riots, which were now three days old. You kept seeing the same blood, the same bodies.

Away in the distance you could hear the occasional gunshot.

We decided we'd stick close to the hotel for a couple of days, follow the news and see how things would develop. Each morning, Evan met with the guide. He'd been out around the streets and had a good idea of how the city was recuperating, what would be safe to do, where we should still avoid.

With all this time to kill, we fished the leaves out of the pool and went swimming. The little guy left in sole charge of the hotel rooted out some tennis gear and we played endless games down on the courts that adjoined the pool. By the end of day two, things seemed to have settled down. The city was slowly getting back to work and the only no-go area left was up around the presidential palace.

The unrest had, of course, made a mess of our itinerary. We shuffled everything around and started scheduling stuff by where in the city it was to be shot. The safest segments now, anything slightly riskier later. And we couldn't leave Venezuela without doing something about the coup itself. That would have been a complete cop-out. Talking it over with the guide, we decided to wait 'til the last day, then head up to the areas that we knew so well from the CNN footage. Turned out we didn't leave it long enough.

Most of the action centred on this flyover, the Puente Llaguna, which overlooks one of the city's busiest streets. We'd seen it a thousand times on TV. These guys with handguns shooting down on the opposing demonstration, crowds of people running at a stoop, trying to escape the crossfire. *Five days later, it was almost as if nothing had happened up there. Almost. The army were still highly visible and there were bullet holes everywhere, in the walls of the buildings, in the roofs and corrugated hoardings. Where did these come from? I shouted up to a woman leaning out of a third-floor window.*

AS THE GUIDE DROVE US IN THROUGH HALF-EMPTY STREETS, **YOU COULD TASTE THE TENSION IN THE AIR. THE MILITARY WERE EVERYWHERE.** POUNDING THE STREETS IN TWOS AND THREES, ARMED TO THE TEETH.

'La metropolitana!' she shouted back. The cops. Chavez supporters were now all over the streets, triumphantly waving Venezuelan flags and copies of the reinstated constitution. The minute they saw the camera, they were up waving the little book in the lens, shouting, 'Viva el presidente!' and punching the air.

We finished shooting and began walking up towards the presidential palace in Miraflores, just up the road from the bridge. Bad idea. Maybe they had been watching us, maybe the passing patrol just didn't like the look of the camera. Whatever the reason, we'd barely left the bridge when these two army jeeps veered off the road and screeched to a halt ahead of us on the path. We froze. Six soldiers, dressed in military fatigues and toting rifles, jumped out. If there's anything more intimidating than a South American soldier in full battledress advancing on you with his rifle cocked, it's six of the fuckers. The head lad starts shouting at us in Spanish. 'What are you doing? What are you doing here!?' I was never so grateful for my four years in the Basque Country. *Esta bien, esta bien*, it's OK, it's OK, I kept saying. I told them we were a TV crew making a tourist programme for Irish TV. He didn't buy it. Weren't there packs of news crews roaming the city covering the coup for international television? Anyone claiming to be a tourist crew in a town where there were fuck-all tourists had to be hiding something. The head lad ripped the camera out of Rosco's arms and herded the three of us into the back of the second jeep. Up the avenue at speed and in through the gates of the palace. Shite. Straight away, Evan got on the phone and called the guide.

We usually run these location shoots like this: the guide drops us where we're doing the shooting, then shadows us in the van where Rosco keeps all his spare tapes, batteries, the tripod and so on. By then, we had it down to a fine art. Jump out, do the piece to camera, jump back in again. Like a combat patrol. This time, though, we misjudged it

'MAYBE THEY HAD BEEN WATCHING US, MAYBE THE PASSING PATROL JUST DIDN'T LIKE THE LOOK OF THE CAMERA. WHATEVER THE REASON, WE'D BARELY LEFT THE BRIDGE WHEN THESE TWO ARMY JEEPS VEERED OFF THE ROAD AND SCREECHED TO A HALT AHEAD OF US ON THE PATH. WE FROZE. SIX SOLDIERS, DRESSED IN MILITARY FATIGUES AND TOTING RIFLES, JUMPED OUT. **IF THERE'S ANYTHING MORE INTIMIDATING THAN A SOUTH AMERICAN SOLDIER IN FULL BATTLEDRESS ADVANCING ON YOU WITH HIS RIFLE COCKED, IT'S SIX OF THE FUCKERS.**'

completely. When Evan called, the guide was streets away. It took him a good ten minutes to get up to the palace. From then on, it was a process of trying to convince the military that we were who we said we were. Evan had an itinerary with all these touristy type things listed out on it. There were the Irish passports. It helped that I looked nothing like a news crew anchor. No flak jacket, no double-breasted suit. No big flash microphone emblazoned with the TG4 logo. Look at us, I kept saying, playing the harmless Paddy card, we're not here for Chavez or the coup, it's only an oul tourist programme. I showed them the stamps on the passports so they could see where we'd been before. 'Here,' says the head lad to Rosco, pushing the camera back into his arms, 'show us what you've shot.'

Ah shite.

Half an hour earlier, we'd interviewed a gang of anti-Chavez heads and got their side of the story. In at the start of that tape was about ten minutes of people going on about what a rotten bastard the president was. But the Sony PD150, thank God, has two rewind buttons, a fast and a slow. Thinking on his feet, Rosco hits the slow, and praying that he hasn't gone too far back, he presses play as the soldiers crowd around the viewfinder. What they get is me walking up the street, doing a piece to camera. I'm summing up the anti-Chavez views we've just recorded, views that these guys have only narrowly missed seeing. And it's all in Irish. God bless the Irish language.

Eventually they cracked, and we got the usual line. Ah, television Irelandesa, eh? Roy Keane, eh? Guinness no? *Muy bien, todo bien*. The soldier threw the camera back into Rosco's arms. 'Lárgate! Fuera de aquí ahora mismo' – basically piss off and don't come back. And if we catch you back here again...

We drove away out the gates of the palace feeling like turkeys on Stephen's Day. Slán agus sábháilte. Right, I said to the driver. 'An aerfort le do thoil.'

MEMPHIS

GRACELAND. First impression, it's much smaller than you'd expect. Looking at footage on TV, you'd think the avenue was a couple of miles long, but it's not. You'd think the house was Áras an Uachtarán, but it isn't. It's big, yeah, but not oh–my–God–will–you–look–at–the–size–of–that–thing big. When Elvis forked out $100,000 for the place back in 1957, it was a grand old mansion out in the country, about twenty miles from Memphis. One of several in what was once the Memphis equivalent of Taylor's Hill or Killiney. Now, of course, the city suburbs have swallowed it up, and the house stands at the centre of this huge electric Elvisland. Across the road you've got the Elvis Love Hotel. There's Elvis–themed restaurants and venues with Elvis impersonators gyrating across the stage day and night. There's the automobile museum, where you can see the trademark Pink Cadillac or climb into his customized Boeing 737. Out the back in his racquetball court, there's the capes and suits in glass cases. Hawaii 1973, Las Vegas 1974. Floor–to–ceiling gold discs. You can buy everything from an Elvis key–ring to an Elvis toilet seat warmer. There's genuine memorabilia where the serious collector can blow his life savings on something the King actually owned. And Graceland itself is the hub of an industry that's still raking in the cash nearly thirty years after that fateful evening when he slid off the toilet and slapped on to the floor.

We arrived at the beginning of Elvis Week. On 16 August, the King would be twenty–six years dead. From the Monday, three days beforehand, the pilgrims began to pile into Memphis. In Winnebagos, mostly, with big, psychedelic Elvis murals on the side. The van would pull into the parking lot and the family would climb down. First the ma. In her fifties. There's a suggestion of Elvis about her, maybe a bit of a lock there below the ear, a bit of a quiff maybe. Then the da. The full-blown Vegas Elvis. The body suit, the belly, the rings, the shades, the boots. Big, fat, quiffed-up hair. All the real deal, of course, no wigs. The son, eighteen, he's got the look as well. The teddy boy. Black leather pants, black leather jacket, white t–shirt, white socks, jet black hair. You'd even see little kids. Eight years old in the white zip suit with the shades and the hair. One hand in the air, giving it the old pelvic thrust.

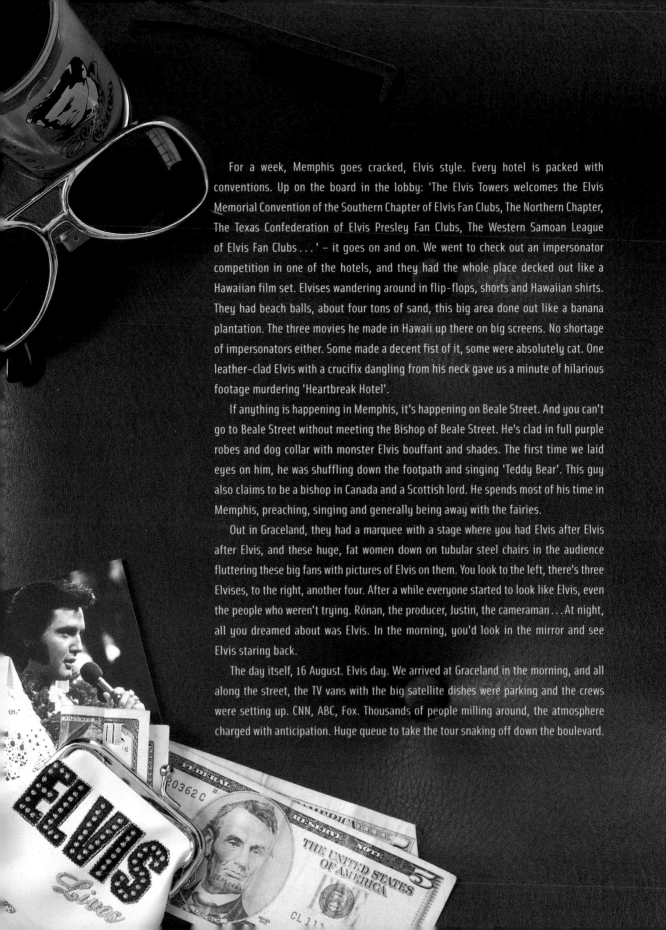

For a week, Memphis goes cracked, Elvis style. Every hotel is packed with conventions. Up on the board in the lobby: 'The Elvis Towers welcomes the Elvis Memorial Convention of the Southern Chapter of Elvis Fan Clubs, The Northern Chapter, The Texas Confederation of Elvis Presley Fan Clubs, The Western Samoan League of Elvis Fan Clubs . . . ' – it goes on and on. We went to check out an impersonator competition in one of the hotels, and they had the whole place decked out like a Hawaiian film set. Elvises wandering around in flip-flops, shorts and Hawaiian shirts. They had beach balls, about four tons of sand, this big area done out like a banana plantation. The three movies he made in Hawaii up there on big screens. No shortage of impersonators either. Some made a decent fist of it, some were absolutely cat. One leather-clad Elvis with a crucifix dangling from his neck gave us a minute of hilarious footage murdering 'Heartbreak Hotel'.

If anything is happening in Memphis, it's happening on Beale Street. And you can't go to Beale Street without meeting the Bishop of Beale Street. He's clad in full purple robes and dog collar with monster Elvis bouffant and shades. The first time we laid eyes on him, he was shuffling down the footpath and singing 'Teddy Bear'. This guy also claims to be a bishop in Canada and a Scottish lord. He spends most of his time in Memphis, preaching, singing and generally being away with the fairies.

Out in Graceland, they had a marquee with a stage where you had Elvis after Elvis after Elvis, and these huge, fat women down on tubular steel chairs in the audience fluttering these big fans with pictures of Elvis on them. You look to the left, there's three Elvises, to the right, another four. After a while everyone started to look like Elvis, even the people who weren't trying. Rónan, the producer, Justin, the cameraman . . . At night, all you dreamed about was Elvis. In the morning, you'd look in the mirror and see Elvis staring back.

The day itself, 16 August. Elvis day. We arrived at Graceland in the morning, and all along the street, the TV vans with the big satellite dishes were parking and the crews were setting up. CNN, ABC, Fox. Thousands of people milling around, the atmosphere charged with anticipation. Huge queue to take the tour snaking off down the boulevard.

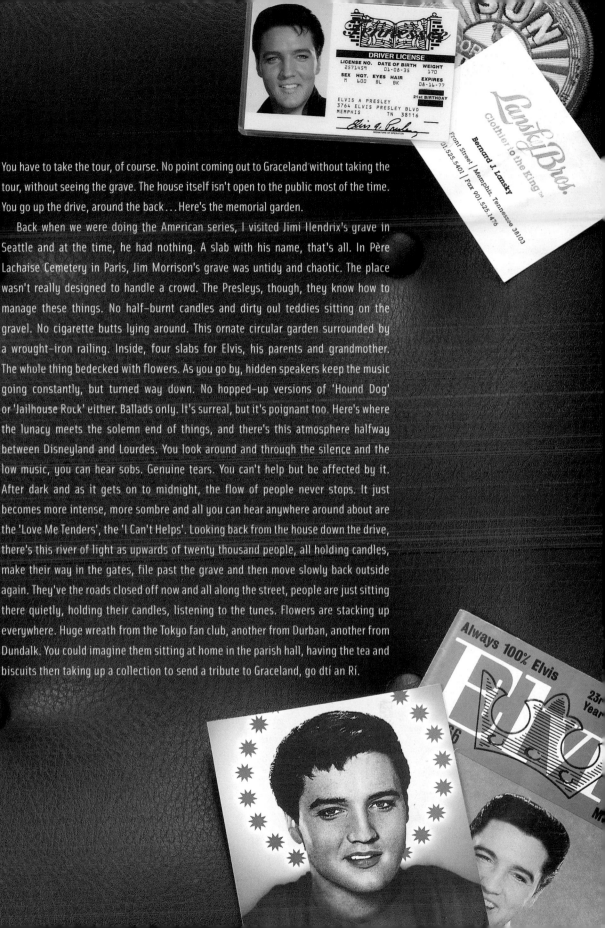

You have to take the tour, of course. No point coming out to Graceland without taking the tour, without seeing the grave. The house itself isn't open to the public most of the time. You go up the drive, around the back... Here's the memorial garden.

Back when we were doing the American series, I visited Jimi Hendrix's grave in Seattle and at the time, he had nothing. A slab with his name, that's all. In Père Lachaise Cemetery in Paris, Jim Morrison's grave was untidy and chaotic. The place wasn't really designed to handle a crowd. The Presleys, though, they know how to manage these things. No half-burnt candles and dirty oul teddies sitting on the gravel. No cigarette butts lying around. This ornate circular garden surrounded by a wrought-iron railing. Inside, four slabs for Elvis, his parents and grandmother. The whole thing bedecked with flowers. As you go by, hidden speakers keep the music going constantly, but turned way down. No hopped-up versions of 'Hound Dog' or 'Jailhouse Rock' either. Ballads only. It's surreal, but it's poignant too. Here's where the lunacy meets the solemn end of things, and there's this atmosphere halfway between Disneyland and Lourdes. You look around and through the silence and the low music, you can hear sobs. Genuine tears. You can't help but be affected by it. After dark and as it gets on to midnight, the flow of people never stops. It just becomes more intense, more sombre and all you can hear anywhere around about are the 'Love Me Tenders', the 'I Can't Helps'. Looking back from the house down the drive, there's this river of light as upwards of twenty thousand people, all holding candles, make their way in the gates, file past the grave and then move slowly back outside again. They've the roads closed off now and all along the street, people are just sitting there quietly, holding their candles, listening to the tunes. Flowers are stacking up everywhere. Huge wreath from the Tokyo fan club, another from Durban, another from Dundalk. You could imagine them sitting at home in the parish hall, having the tea and biscuits then taking up a collection to send a tribute to Graceland, go dtí an Rí.

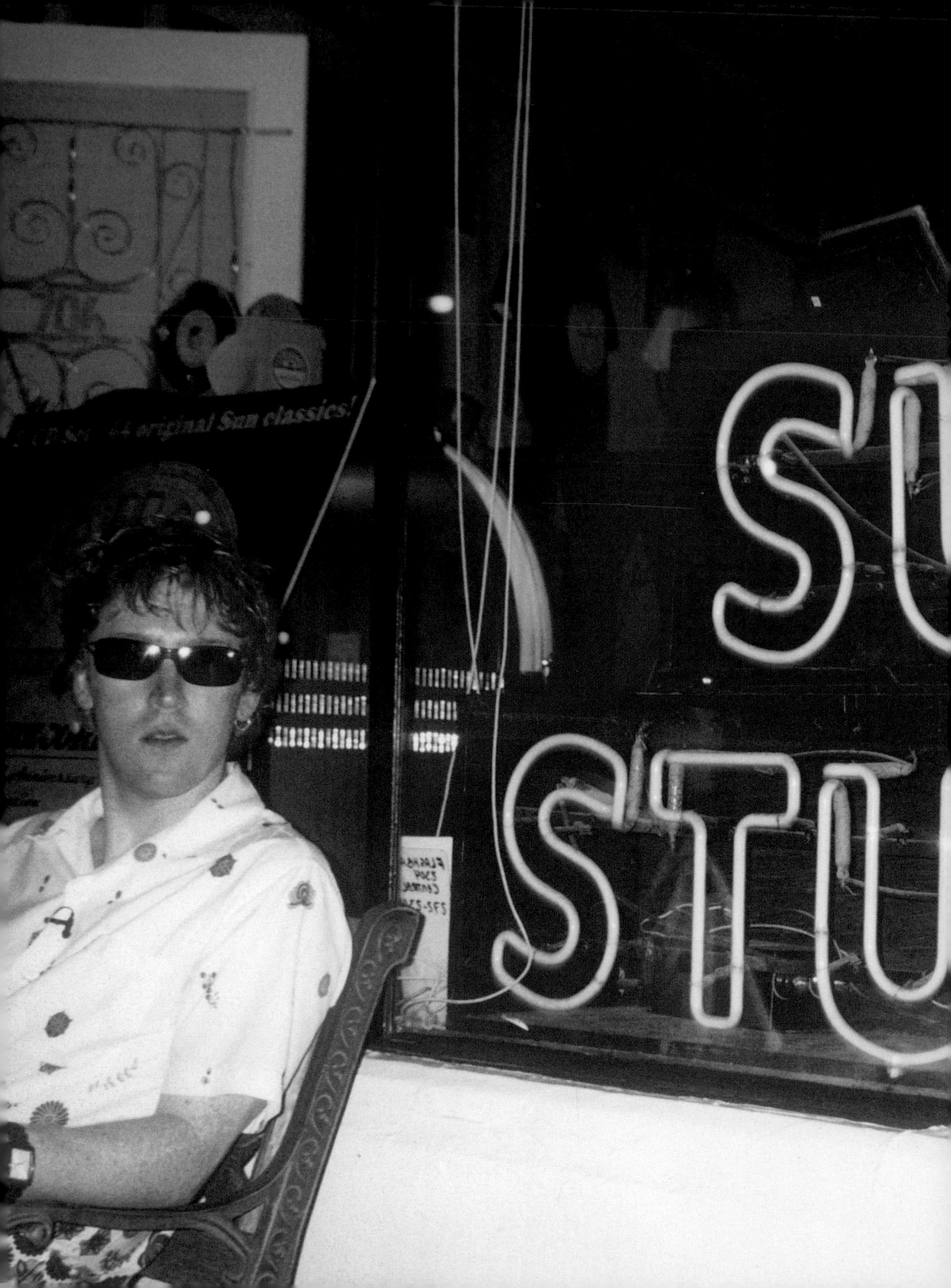
44 original Sun classics!

Sun Studios. Myself and Dympna spent ages trying to pick the right song. We eventually settled on 'Devil In Disguise' because of that snappy little tempo change in the middle. Recording in Sun Studios was a real thrill. Back in 1953, when it was still known as the Memphis Recording Service, Elvis showed up with four dollars to record 'Mr Happiness' as a present for his mother. A couple of months later, when he came back to do another, Sam Philips happened to be there. And that was that. They've all these old black-and-white photos on the wall: Elvis, Johnny Cash, Jerry Lee Lewis, Carl Perkins. That familiar yellow Sun logo out front. The two boys got to record there too. Rónan, who's a great singer, did 'In The Ghetto'. But Justin's version of 'Devil In Disguise' was cat. He'd have been better off reading it as a poem. The lad hasn't got a note in his head or a beat in his body.

Afterwards, we went up to Lansky Brothers, the clothes shop where Elvis used to buy all his gear. Old Mr Lansky, now eighty-four years old, is still behind the counter, full of Elvis stories. 'Dynamite guy,' he says of the King. 'A real gentleman.' *An lá tar éis lá an Rí, 17 August is my birthday, so I picked up a couple of rockabilly style T-Bird shirts. Tell you what. They look horrid cool under the UV lights in the Palace Niteclub in Navan.*

'SUN STUDIOS. MYSELF AND DYMPNA SPENT AGES TRYING TO PICK THE RIGHT SONG. WE EVENTUALLY SETTLED ON 'DEVIL IN DISGUISE' BECAUSE OF THAT SNAPPY LITTLE TEMPO CHANGE IN THE MIDDLE. **RECORDING IN SUN STUDIOS WAS A REAL THRILL.**'

'AH, SUE ELLEN. SHE WAS THE ONE FOR ME. LUCY MIGHT HAVE BEEN A SAUCY LITTLE VIXEN, BUT I DIDN'T LIKE THAT RAPUNZEL, HAIR DOWN TO HER ARSE. YOU'LL NEVER FORGET THOSE CHARACTERS: JR THE SCHEMER, RAY THE CATTLE-WRANGLER, BOBBY WITH THE WEBBED HANDS, CLIFF BARNES THE DOPE,

DALLAS

SOUTHFORK WAS A BIT OF A CON. They never filmed a single frame inside the house. It was all done in studios a thousand miles away in Hollywood. Only the exterior shots were taken here. The ranch itself, about twenty-five miles north of Dallas, is just like you remember it. The arched gateway, the long drive up, the big, old, rambling house and the flat, empty fields surrounding it all. Up near the road they've converted one of Ray Krebb's haggards into a museum where they have glass cases full of stuff like Lucy's wedding dress, JR's hat and Miss Ellie's dentures.

Here's where I met Sally, our guide. Big plum pudding of a woman, dressed in bright crimson with a voice like a bullhorn. 'Hi, how are ya! Welcome to Southfork, Hector! Oh, honey we're so happy to have you today!' The entire time we were there, she did not pause to draw breath but kept myself and the rest of the tour entertained with an endless stream of useless information. 'It was right here at this spot that Sue Ellen discovered she was with child...It was with this very boot that Bobby kicked JR in the balls in episode forty-two...Here's the pitchfork that became lodged in Ray's ass while he and Lucy were frolicking in the hay barn...' They have this 'tram' to bring the tourists from the museum down to the house itself, but it's no more than a little tractor with a few trailers on the back. 'Hi, my name's Gary, and I'll be your tram driver today. Please fasten your seatbelts and keep your hands in from the sides.' The stupid thing only goes four miles an hour.

Down at the house, Sally's got a little seminar going. She gives us all the stats about the success of the show, the number of episodes, the fans, the languages it's been dubbed into and all the rest of it. For me, like so many others, *Dallas* was one of the highlights of the week. Myself and the two brothers drying in front of the fire after the bath. These days you've all kinds of vitamin supplements and tonics for kids, but in Navan in the mid-eighties, we had Radiomulsion. Thick, yellow, sweety stuff in a huge brown bottle. Mam would give us each a spoon, then once the nine o'clock news was over, the announcer came on, and the music started up. Ah, Sue Ellen. She was the one for me. Leaning up against the fireplace, clinking the ice in her glass. 'JR, I wanna divorce.' Pam left me cold. She was just too nice. Lucy might have been a saucy little vixen, but I didn't like that Rapunzel, hair down to her arse. You'll never forget those characters: JR the schemer, Ray the cattle-wrangler, Bobby with the webbed hands, Cliff Barnes the dope.

There are signs all over the house saying don't sit here, don't stand there, but I keep slipping away from the tour so's we can get some footage of me grinding away up on JR's duvet, lounging in Lucy's Jacuzzi. 'He did some damage there,' I say to Sally, indicating the bed, but it goes over her head. She's standing at the window, pointing. 'Jock took a crap behind that bush.' Despite the fact that nothing was ever shot inside the house, they've the whole place got up 'in the style of *Dallas*'. You've signs up for things like 'Miss Ellie's Rose Garden Bedroom', but none of it looks anything like the show used to.

Up on the veranda, you could see where the cars used to come sweeping down the drive. And, of course, here's the pool. Sue Ellen doing the backstroke. Those big, quivering lips. O Sea, Sue Ellen. Sin é, SIN É! Níos Mó! Níos Mó, Sue Ellen. Arís! Arís! Seaaaaaaaaa!

'WHAT WE'D HEARD WAS THAT THERE WAS A LAD IN TAIPEI WHO WOULD STAND ON A COUPLE OF DOZEN EGGS WITHOUT BREAKING THEM, THEN PAINT A PICTURE. WE HADN'T HEARD THAT HIMSELF AND NINETEEN OF HIS STUDENTS WERE GEARING UP FOR A WORLD RECORD ATTEMPT. **THEY WANTED TO SEE HOW FAR THEY COULD PULL A JUMBO JET HARNESSED TO THEIR TWENTY MICKEYS.**'

TAIWAN

SOMETIMES YOU SPEND WEEKS PREPARING FOR SOMETHING. There's faxes back and forth, phone calls to confirm; you plan and talk about it over and over again. Then, on the day, it falls flat on its arse. The people are dull, the story isn't half as good as it appeared on paper. Something just doesn't click. Other times, though, it works the other way round, and that's just brilliant. Walking up to Mr Tu's that Monday night, I'd no idea that a few months later, I'd be standing in the wings at *The Late Late Show*, listening to Pat Kenny introduce the footage we were about to shoot. Or that it would win us an IFTA for the best show of 2003. Or that I was about to dangle a five-kilogram weight from my mickey.

It was towards the end of our five days in Taiwan, and what we had in the bag wasn't exactly mind-blowing. I'd checked out the sulphur baths on the outskirts of the city, and there was a temple where a holy woman with hiccups cleansed my aura. They had these twenty-four-hour bookshops that'd be packed in the dead of night while the nightclubs were empty. We went cruising for glic-chicks in the Taipei equivalent of Easons at one in the morning on the Saturday.

Evan, who has a nose for this sort of thing, had ferreted out our Master Tu. He had been an Olympic and World champion in his day; now he was a full-time martial arts instructor. But he had this quirky side. What we'd heard was that there was a lad in Taipei who would stand on a couple of dozen eggs without breaking them, then paint a picture. We hadn't heard that himself and nineteen of his students were gearing up for a world record attempt. They wanted to see how far they could pull a jumbo jet harnessed to their twenty mickeys.

That night we arrived into an ordinary slice of Taiwanese life. Students, suits, loads of
IT heads – ordinary lads coming in from work to catch their Monday evening Tai Chi class.
It might have been the local parish hall at home. We took off our shoes like the rest and
hung back for a bit, watching Master Tu patrol these lines of students like a sergeant major.
We were told he was around fifty-five, but he looked twenty years younger. Thick-set and
serious as befuck, like Oddjob in James Bond except with hair. He'd stop here and there
along the row, draw back the fist and bang! Sock the lad into the gut. Each man stood there
with this intense, constipated look on his face, channelling all his Chi against Tu's blows.
Next, he took a bunch of chopsticks and went back through the lines again, stabbing the
boys in the belly with the sticks until they splintered and broke. Nobody buckled in pain.
Nobody broke ranks.

After a while we copped that there was a fair bit of showmanship going on. The class was
about halfway through when an assistant appeared with two big trays of eggs and brought
them up to me. 'Please please. Break, break!' He wanted me to poke a finger through a few,
make sure they weren't all made out of cast iron. I jabbed a couple at random. Ordinary
eggs. Not even hardboiled. They put the two trays down on the floor, then brought out an
easel and set it up. Tu, his feet and legs bound up in padded shoes, eased himself gently up
on top of the eggs. As he held this awkward stance like a water-skier, they handed him the
paintbrush, and off he went. In no time at all he had painted this beautiful country scene.
Bamboo and grass with graceful Chinese lettering down the side. Afterwards, we inspected
the eggs, and there wasn't so much as a crack in any of them.

But there was this back-room. I'd noticed it at the start. People wandering in and out.
The good stuff is always in the back-room.

We didn't have to ask. Mr Tu led us in there – we'd no Chinese, of course, and he'd no English – but one of the lads out of the class had just enough to interpret. There was nothing remarkable about the room itself, nothing to indicate what went on in there. There were the weights, of course, stacked on top of each other with these short metal hooks rising up out of them. I suppose the oddest thing about it was the paunchy middle-aged chap standing in the middle of the floor in the Hakka stance, going 'Awwwwww chi!' and thumping himself in the stomach. He was wearing a pale-blue skirt.

Our new interpreter brings me over to him. No introduction or anything. 'OK, please, sir, hit, hit!' Sorry? What do you want me to do? 'Please, sir, hit. Hit!' He indicates that he wants me to punch your man in the stomach. He, meanwhile, is bracing himself for a belt. I look back at Rosco, who shrugs, so I give your man a playful tap with the back of the hand. The interpreter shakes his head impatiently. 'No, no, sir, hit! Hit!'

Hang on there a minute now, I said, I'm not going to hit him. 'No, sir, hit! Hit!' Your man in the skirt is punctuating these requests for violence with more of this 'Aawwwwww chi! He looks at me expectantly, the belly stuck out like a burst football. I hit him a bit harder. Rosco looks out from behind the camera and says 'Will you fuckin' hit him, will you?' For fuck's sake, Rosco, I said, I'm not going to hit him. The interpreter is getting excited now and becomes even more insistent. 'No, sir, please, hit, HIT!'

OK, OK. Nobody was going to be happy – including your man himself – until I leathered him in the belly. So I bunch the fist, draw back and hit him the hardest I can. Sweet Jesus, the pain. Like hitting a concrete wall. Your man is there grinning, not a bother on him, but inside two minutes, my knuckles are black and blue and starting to swell. Mr Tu, now suddenly playing the perfect host, brings me back to the main room and spends the next fifteen minutes massaging my knuckles. Through the interpreter, he tells me that it's possible to deflate bruising if you work on it quickly. I'd never seen anything like it. In quarter of an hour, the knuckles are back to normal, and the discoloration has been pushed up into the back of my hand.

'OK, OK. NOBODY WAS GOING TO BE HAPPY – INCLUDING YOUR MAN HIMSELF – UNTIL I LEATHERED HIM IN THE BELLY. SO I BUNCH THE FIST, DRAW BACK AND HIT HIM THE HARDEST I CAN. SWEET JESUS, THE PAIN. LIKE HITTING A CONCRETE WALL. YOUR MAN IS THERE GRINNING, NOT A BOTHER ON HIM, BUT INSIDE TWO MINUTES, MY KNUCKLES ARE BLACK AND BLUE AND STARTING TO SWELL.'

Turns out your man in the skirt has been a student of Tu's for the past eight months. He came to the master to seek help for a problem common in men of his age. The droopy lad. An leaid lag. Tu had prescribed a rigorous programme of exercise for the affected area. Oh yeah? I said. What's that? I'll show you, says Tu. Back into the back room again, where your man is now straddling two massive weights stacked on top of each other like poker chips. He now has a silk rope dangling from between his legs and he's there looping the end of it over the hooked metal rod that rises from the centre of the two discs.

Is he?

I mean, can he be?

Is that?

Tell us, I lean over to the interpreter, is he doing what I think he's doing?

'Eighty kilo!' The interpreter grins.

A little more awwww chi-ing and the chap in the skirt takes the strain. It's a nasty sight, watching that rope go taut. Sheeeeeee-Uh! Eighty kilos are jerked – jerked! – from the floor and swing gently from the lad's lad. That's the weight of a bull calf. A good, strong bull calf.

It was a night of several firsts. I'd never asked a man to lift his skirt before for a start. Obliging chap that he was, I didn't have to ask twice, and he continues to display it proudly as Rosco moves in for the money shot. Of course, when it came time to broadcast, TG4 decided the sight of an Asian lad all trussed up in blue silk was a too much for the viewing public, so they pixelated it out.

Ah-ha! says I. The mickey alone does not bear the weight but shares it with the entire tackle. You hauls balls and all down and make your knot up there where the mála agus na liathroidí join the rest of the body.

Does it hurt? Your man shakes the head. You kind of get the impression that even if it did he'd never admit it.

'You try?' says the interpreter.

Now. Bungee-jumping, para-gliding, abseiling. None of this shit appeals to me. Where's the sense in jumping out of a perfectly functioning aeroplane? But dangling a few kilos from the lad? That's funny. If I was sitting at home on the couch and I flicked on the television on a Friday night, that'd make me laugh. So I said, yeah, I'd give it a lash. While I go scouting for the lightest weight in the room, my friend of the eighty kilos gets a little cocky. He loops on a piddling five kilos and starts swinging it between his legs like a metronome. Stupid Irishman, I could do this all day! But that size – five kilos – was as low as they went, so it was on with the skirt (another first) and off with the fobhrístí. Refusing the interpreter's eager offer of help – there are some doors a man must pass through alone – I get your man to show me again how the knot is done. Warm it up they said, so I did the little plasticine rub, shizzsha shizzsha shizzsha… Then it was a case of keeping Rosco at bay while I gently tied the crucial knot.

There'd be no jerking this time. I positioned myself over the weight, looped the silk rope over the hook and slowly began to straighten up. Downstairs, things began to stretch. Slowly, slowly, taking care that the strain was bearable, the weight lifted off the floor.

This was ten days after we'd finished the Bali programme, when I'd got the name of the show henna-tattooed on my backside. Only that day I'd discovered that, though the henna had faded, the skin had become seriously inflamed and you could still read the words Amú San Áise in angry, itchy red where the henna used to be. The upshot of all this was that I now stood in a back room in downtown Taipei with a rash on my arse and five kilos dangling from my lad. Oh yes, and wearing a fetching green silk skirt.

All in a day's work.

Still and all though, probably the highlight of the whole thing was Pat Kenny asking me what was the Irish for scrotum. The same, I told him, only with a fada over the O.

THERE'D BE NO JERKING THIS TIME. I POSITIONED MYSELF OVER THE WEIGHT, LOOPED THE SILK ROPE OVER THE HOOK AND SLOWLY BEGAN TO STRAIGHTEN UP. DOWNSTAIRS, THINGS BEGAN TO STRETCH. SLOWLY, SLOWLY, TAKING CARE THAT THE STRAIN WAS BEARABLE, THE WEIGHT LIFTED OFF THE FLOOR.

BEER BIBLE

>>> Bali – Bintang

A carefully chosen mix of grains combine to produce a subtle balance of flavours, simultaneously suggestive of mellow autumnal sunsets and cat piss. KEEPS YOU COOL WHILE HAVING YOUR ARSE TATTOOED.

>>> Thailand – Singha

At 6%, IT KICKS LIKE AN ASIAN MULE. So beware. Unsuspecting Irish lads who end up with ladyboys tend to blame Singha for hijacking their ability to tell a buachaill from a cailín.

>>> Brazil – Brahma

BUDWEISER WITH A BRAZILIAN ACCENT. Rough and all as that sounds, this is a nice light, summery beer, excellent for drinking while sitting on Copacabana beach slathered in factor 400, fully dressed and shaded by an enormous sun umbrella. We redheads take no chances.

>>> Costa Rica – Imperial

SIMPLY THE FINEST BEER I'VE EVER HAD. Tastes as good on the fourth as it does on the first. How many beers can you say that about?

>>> Japan – Asahi

A PALE, DRY SORT OF BEER, kind of like the Japanese themselves.

>>> Bolivia – Paceña

MMMMMMMM. YUMMY. Careful though. La Paz being the highest capital city the world, the altitude will get you scuttered on a fraction of what it usually takes.

>>> Jamaica – Red Stripe

LILT FOR GROWN-UPS. You haven't lived til you've sat with your back against a mango tree, a can of Red Stripe in one hand and a big fat, ah, packet of Tayto Cheese and Onion crisps in the other.

>>> Argentina – Quilmes

Me encanta el Quilmes! Makes you realize that the beer we pour into ourselves over here is just chemical soup. This stuff is perfect. PLENTY OF BITE, NO AFTERTASTE. The perfect accompaniment to one Quilmes is a second one. Then a third. And while we're at it, why not another...?

>>> Singapore Airlines – Tiger

So called because the following day, you'll feel like you've been mauled by a big cat. NOTHING BETTER to chase the Muslim blues away when you're leaving alcohol-free Brunei. Pretty much drank the plane dry on our way to Manila.

>>> Nashville – Bud Light

PISS. Gets you drunk though.

ADRENALIN

GREAT FUN – UNTIL SOMEONE WINDS UP IN A SOUTH AMERICAN JAIL, GETS GORED BY A BULL OR IS JUMPED BY IRATE SOCCER FANS: TERROR WITH A NAVAN ACCENT

ARGENTINA

YOU DEVELOP A SIXTH SENSE FOR TROUBLE. The minute the camera comes out of the bag, you know whether or not it's going to work. Filming in public, you have to put up with a certain amount of interruption, fair enough. Kids grinning in the background, doing the rabbit ears with their fingers. Lads at the races in behind you with the mobile phone: 'Turn on the telly! Turn on the telly! I'm on the telly!' Mostly it's just harmless fun, sometimes you can even use it, but sometimes it's got that nasty little undercurrent, that aggressive edge.

So we watch each other's backs. Rosco is the most vulnerable. He's bent over the camera, concentrating on the shot, often walking backwards. I'm keeping an eye on what's going on around him while Evan, twenty yards away, watches me.

On the South American trip, three places stuck out. The first was Mexico City, in the Zocalo, the main square. The city has one of the worst crime records in the world. Besides the poverty – families sleeping in ATM lobbies, street kids chasing you trying to sell you stuff – there's an underlying aggression, like a fight could break out any minute. As we walked up to the square, there was this group of young lads watching our approach. I heard one of them turn to his mate and sneer at us in Spanish: 'Fucking Americans. Here they come with their fucking cameras.' I went straight over and started talking to them in Spanish, told them we weren't American, we were Irish, but they weren't interested. American, Irish, it was all the one. Gringos. Foreign. Unwelcome.

Rio was another dodgy spot. We didn't get any night-time footage here for the same reason. The minute the camera came out, they started pushing Rosco, there were boys jumping out in front of the lens. It was something more than drunken high

spirits, something more than just young lads having a laugh. You can't take them on, you can't try to soldier on, you just have to shut down and get out.

Then there was La Boca, the Buenos Aires suburb where Boca Juniors play their football. One of the most famous football clubs on the planet and the spiritual home of one Diego Armando Maradona. He got his start here and still keeps a box high up in the centre of the main stand. They showed us the four yellow chairs where Diego and his family come to watch home games.

In hindsight, the timing of our visit couldn't have been worse. We were still on a high from Brazil and flew in from the tropical rhythms of Rio to a city on the edge of winter and in the middle of an economic crisis. It rained most of the time we were there. Walking down the street, you could sense the depression. No smiles, no banter. The shops were empty. We went into this huge, four-storey sports megastore on the main street. Everything was on special offer, everything was reduced to clear, but we were the only people in it. Out on the street, you'd pass these huge demonstrations every five minutes. People out in front of banks banging pots and pans, making the most godawful clatter. The banks themselves were all encased in six-inch steel and looked more like military installations than anything else. All were plastered with angry graffiti. Earlier in the year, after a decade of dodgy economics, confidence in the peso plummeted. Foreign banks pulled out, and people began changing their own money into dollars. The government responded by effectively freezing everybody's account. It didn't matter how much money you had in the bank, you were only allowed to draw out a tiny amount per week. At the same time, they abandoned legislation that tied the peso to the dollar. The value of the currency dropped like a stone. If you had peso savings, they were now worth a fraction of what they had been. If you had a dollar loan, you suddenly had to pay back way more than you borrowed.

In was in this angry, frustrated atmosphere that we made our trip out to La Boca, one of the most colourful, but also one of the poorest, areas of the city.

Now, everybody knows they take their football seriously in South America. But in La Boca, there is nothing except football. The stadium, La Bombonera, is the heartbeat of the community. Everything revolves around it. Derbies between themselves and arch enemies River Plate make the Old Firm rivalry look like a lovers' tiff. On one infamous occasion during the nineties, River Plate beat Boca 3–1. That night, two River Plate fans were stabbed to death. A Boca fan, interviewed on TV afterwards, said, 'That makes it three-all.' Both clubs were founded in La Boca, but River Plate moved to the Buenos Aires equivalent of Killiney in the 1930s. So besides the football, this perception of it being about rich versus poor stokes the whole thing up even more.

'APPROACHING LA TRECE, I COULD SENSE THAT THIS WAS SOMETHING I HADN'T EXPERIENCED BEFORE. THESE GUYS WERE JUST WATCHING A MATCH ON TV, BUT THE INTENSITY OF THE PLACE WAS SOMETHING ELSE. THE SMELLS OF THE TERRACE: **HASH, SWEAT. BODIES PRESSED CLOSE TOGETHER. THE CHANTING. THERE WAS SOMETHING RADICALLY DIFFERENT ABOUT THE CHANTING.**

The week we were there, the team were playing away from home, in the Copa de Libertadores – their Champions League. But in La Bombonera, they were still expecting something in the region of 25,000 fans. The morning we went out to see the team train, they were putting up TVs and big screens to cater for the crowd that would be in to watch the match that night.

We were dealing with this slick, flamboyant publicist. He presented me with the new-season jersey – which got robbed along with all my other football jerseys somewhere between Buenos Aires and Dublin – and promised us all kinds of access to the team. But in the end, we got precious little. I'd brought my gear, hoping to get down and train with them. No way. A TV presenter kicking football? Too weird for these lads. Watching the team at work, there were only a couple of faces I recognized. Juan Roman Riquelme, their star midfielder, also the only Argentine international who still played at home. Not for long, though. Only that morning, I'd read in the local paper that he'd just put in for a transfer. Earlier in the year, his brother Christian had been kidnapped, and Riquelme paid over $325,000 to get him back. He said that he and his family were living in constant fear, that they'd had enough and wanted out.

Heading back into La Boca that night, the atmosphere was warm and upbeat. Because it was all the one team, there was no security, no cops, no horses. I picked up a Boca hat in one of the stalls outside and, as we filmed the introduction to the section, there was a lot of laddish lepping around in front of the camera. Nothing dodgy, nothing more than you'd expect. The plan was to head down to La Trece. The Thirteen. This is where the hardcore fans go, the local Boca boys, the equivalent of the Stretford End, Hill 16, the Kop. As we climbed the steps towards the terraces, there were teams of women lined up inside the steel banisters, holding open large black rubbish bags. The fans streaming past tossed in packets of rice, spaghetti, tins of soup. There were no tickets tonight. Instead, you brought food that would be distributed to those hit hardest by the economic collapse. Proof, if it were needed, of just how shitty things had become.

Approaching La Trece, I could sense that this was something I hadn't experienced before. These guys were just watching a match on TV, but the intensity of the place was

something else. The smells of the terrace: hash, sweat. Bodies pressed close together. The chanting. There was something radically different about the chanting.

A couple of years ago, we brought Pete Boyle, the guy who makes up all the Manchester United chants, over to Galway and had a great night in the Radisson with about two hundred fans, singing the songs. Most of these chants, they're sarcastic, they're funny. 'Giggs, Giggs will tear you apart again', 'When Johnny goes marching down the wing, O'Shea, O'Shea'. Harmless fun, most of it. Some people sing them, some don't. But up in La Troce, all five thousand fans were standing with their arms in the air, moving in perfect unison, belting out these chants like they were mantras, like their lives depended on it. Everyone. No exceptions. It was tribal, it was primitive. It was like at any minute, they'd wheel out the virgin and toss her into the volcano.

Ours is a hands-on show. We don't just take our pictures and comment on whatever's going on from a distance. I get in among the crowd. That's how it works. So in I went, down the front, up against the forty-foot steel wire of the bullpen.

The minute Rosco bends over the viewfinder, the pushing starts. It's just young lads, sixteen-year-old gurriers, but that doesn't make the going any easier. The noise is incredible. I have to shout into the camera. Evan is standing back, trying to keep out of shot, but he's starting to get nervous. The match has only kicked off when I hear them for the first time. Shouts in Spanish from back up the terrace. 'Get out of here, motherfucker.' More pushing. There's not much happening on the screen and more and more people start focusing on us. I'm trying to get involved, show I'm on their side. I've got the jersey, I've got the hat, I'm shouting for Boca. This cuts no ice. All we're getting is hostility. A sudden shove from the back and someone swipes the hat. Down in the front, Rosco is getting pushed more aggressively. Someone comes up and spits in the lens. Suddenly, on the TV screen, Boca make a break up the pitch and everyone rushes to the front. They don't give a fuck who's in the way. I've seen footage of what happens when they score. The place goes berserk. Hundreds of them hit the wire and start climbing. I'm thinking of the camera. If the camera gets hit, if the camera gets broken, if we have to go looking for a replacement, we could be stuck here for weeks. There's a shot, that in-drawn breath of a crowd all praying for the same thing . . . But it's wide. The mob recedes back up the terrace like a wave. Next thing two young fellas jump me. The jersey. They're trying to pull the jersey off. I drag myself away, trying not to make too much of it, trying not to antagonize them.

That's when it hits me. Of course they don't want us here. We're foreigners, we're trespassing on sacred ground. This is their place, and here we are some gringo TV crew. I'm wearing the brand new team jersey. No one else has one. It's not even in the shops, not that it would matter if it was because there's fuck-all money to go buying expensive football kit. They were collecting food at the turnstiles for Christ's sake. There's no megastore downstairs, no Boca TV, no huge merchandising operation.

Another surge up the pitch, the wrong way this time. Shot. Goal. You can sense a whole new wave of anger flood into the terrace behind us. We just shouldn't be here. This is the wrong time and the wrong place. After twenty minutes, Evan pulls the plug. 'Come on,' he says, 'let's get out of here.' Rosco throws the camera back in the bag and we edge our way out of La Trece while the crowd vents its fury into the air. We finish the night with some footage in one of the main stands, where there are kids and families and granddads, where we can look over into the madness we've left from a safe distance. The intensity never ebbs through the whole night. Five thousand people chanting and pointing at the TV screens in front of them.

In the end Boca go down by that one goal. We wait in the main building until the crowd has gone, then send for the van to come and pick us up.

'PAMPLONA, A SLEEPY LITTLE PROVINCIAL TOWN FOR MOST OF THE YEAR, GOES INSANE FOR SEVEN DAYS IN JULY. THE PUBS STAY OPEN, THE SANGRIA FLOWS, THE MUSIC PUMPS OUT, THERE'S DANCING ON TABLES, SINGING IN THE STREETS, PEOPLE THROWING UP IN CORNERS OR CURLED UP ASLEEP ON THE FOOTPATH**'**

PAMPLONA

LAS FIESTAS DE SAN FERMÍN. THE FAMOUS BULL-RUNNING FESTIVAL IN PAMPLONA. Working in Spain in the mid-nineties, I used to watch it live on TV each morning before I went out to work. They covered it like any other sports event. You'd have a correspondent down on the street talking about ground conditions, another in the enclosure discussing the bulls. You'd have helicopters in the sky for the aerial views and neat little graphics showing the danger spots, where the serious injuries happened the day before. Then, at eight o'clock on the button, the firework goes off, and six wild bulls explode from the gates at Santo Domingo. You get four minutes of Basque lunacy as upwards of two thousand runners sprint their living best down narrow cobbled streets that twist and turn treacherously, while the bulls tear down after them.

This is how the Spanish party.

Pamplona, a sleepy little provincial town for most of the year, goes insane for seven days in July. The pubs stay open, the sangria flows, the music pumps out, there's dancing on tables, singing in the streets, people throwing up in corners or curled up asleep on the footpath. A dangerous business, this. A couple of years ago, two Americans were chopped to pieces by a street sweeper. Passed out amid the debris of the piss-up, the guy never spotted them and they got sucked into the machine. Everyone's knocking back huge *katxis* of Kalimotxo, a powerful mixture of wine and Coke – the Basque equivalent of Buckfast. You've Irish boys staggering arm in arm around the streets, party girls from Madrid stoked up on coke and amphetamines, Australian extreme sports heads eating their energy bars and drinking their coffee, Americans in raingear thumbing through guide books and Japanese couples weighed down with four different types of camera. For twenty-three hours and fifty minutes each day, anything

goes. Then, at seven-fifty in the morning, the bar managers shut off the music, pull down the shutters and close the doors. The strangest kind of tension creeps over the town as everyone takes up positions along the street. As the second hand closes on eight o'clock, all eyes turn towards the gates at Santo Domingo, the firework goes off, and out come the bulls.

In four minutes, it's over. The shutters go up, the DJs get back to work, and the drinking, dancing, singing and puking continue as if they'd never stopped.

I arrived in Pamplona undecided. To run or not to run. If something's fun, I'll give it a lash, but Jackass TV this ain't. No one ever died as a result of drinking frog milkshakes or dangling weights from their mickey. But fourteen people have been gored to death on the streets of Pamplona over the past eighty years. And it's getting more and more dangerous by the year. Popularity is the problem. Everybody wants to say they've done it. The extreme sports boys have added it to their list. Stag parties are organized around it. You'll see whole squads of English chaps flown in on packages from Manchester and London, boasting about how close they got to the animals. One thousand men packed like sardines on the narrow streets as six wild bulls come careering down the cobbles is a scary prospect. Three thousand half-scuttered, unfit daytrippers makes it a whole lot worse. And I'd been watching it for years. I knew what these bulls were capable of. Five hundred kilos, each one. Horns that extend two foot either side of a head that's four times the size of Mike Tyson's. Six turned loose on to the street, tens of thousands of people screaming at them from the walls, this huge press of people taunting them from the front. I'd seen people tossed on those horns like puppets, seen them stretched out in hospital the following day with broken legs, punctured rectums, slashed stomachs, eighteen-inch wounds. I'd seen the blood on the cobbles.

So I staked out the route, studied the danger points, picked out the best place to run from and the best escape points.

This really is what it's all about. Seasoned runners have their favourite spots where they wait 'til the last minute, 'til the bulls are nearly on top of them. The aim is to get in among the animals, to actually run with the bulls. You stay fifty, seventy, a hundred yards at best, then get out to the side and leap the barrier.

Locals, the guys hardwired to the culture of the run, they make up the core of the pack. You'll have fathers and sons, workmates, guys who'll get up and do it before breakfast, then head off to work for the day. These guys, dressed in the traditional red and white, gather before the small statue of San Fermín at the top of Calle Santiago from seven-thirty. Waving their rolled-up newspapers – the only weapon you're allowed on the run – at the statue, they'll chant and sing, asking the saint to protect them through the coming four minutes of mayhem. The real hardcore boys, mostly Basques, they station themselves fifty yards from the Santo Domingo gates, which is as close as the cops let you go. The Australian and American Jackass merchants, sober and fit and wearing the Assic Gel Rebok Marathon ultra runners, are next along. They're taking it as seriously as the Basques, but the attitude couldn't be more different. For the Pamplonese, this is maintaining a tradition that they can trace back to the thirteenth century. Yeah, it's macho, it's dangerous, it's cracked, but it's what their padres did, what their padres' padres did. It means something more than a notch in the belt, the latest adrenalin-fuelled joyride.

Then it's the rabble. The mix of tourists of all nationalities, pumped to the gills on pills, beer, sangria and adrenalin. As zero hour approaches, the chat gets more and more edgy. Boys are sobering up and thinking twice. They're pacing the route, rechecking exit strategies, compulsively watching the clock . . . At about six-fifteen, a squad of about fifty Spanish police begin walking up through the pack, which by now is strung out almost along the entire route. Their job is to root out the lads who are just too wasted to manage it. Once upon a time they pulled the girls out of it too. Now, they leave the handful alone. The cops make sure no one's carrying bottles or backpacks; anything bulky, anything that could possibly be used as a weapon against the bulls. Give these lads half an excuse and you'll be out over the barrier as quick as if you were tossed out by one of the bulls themselves.

Once I'd worked out my plan of campaign, walked and rewalked the course a couple of times, I decided OK, I'd do it.

This thing, it's not really about being the fastest runner. Yes, if you've a turn of speed, great, it'll stand you in good stead, but slip on the cobbles, trip over a lace, and you're fucked. Ten yards ahead of you, someone goes down, someone else trips over him, next thing there's a pile-up. The bulls won't step politely round a pile-up.

THE GOLDEN RULE: if you go down, stay down. Start to get up, the bull will see you. He'll see you and he'll have something to aim at.

It goes against every natural impulse to stay stock still while 500 kilos of bovine fury is bearing down at you, but it's the only way to stay safe.

Within an hour of the end of the run, the photos are up in the town hall. You'll see it there. The head of a bull cocked at an angle as some airborne Australian fool is wishing to Jaysus he'd stuck to para-gliding. I saw it happen to a lad earlier in the week. He was pressed against the wall at the corner as the bulls turned into the Plaza de Toros – you've never seen fear 'til you've seen some lad trying to make himself as small as possible in a doorway on Calle Estafeta as the bulls come sliding round the corner. This guy, he was lucky. The bulls never spotted him. Delighted with himself, he punches the air, lets a out few shouts, then off he goes after the bull closest to him and starts poking at its head with his paper.

The bull turns.

This is what everybody is warned about. Any time a bull breaks from the herd and starts back up towards Santo Domingo, there's carnage. Hundreds of runners are still out on the streets following them down. These are herding animals, and if one becomes separated from the others, he becomes disoriented and pissed off in the extreme. In this case, the bull concentrated on the Australian who'd taunted him. The photo in the town hall the next day showed your man's face twisted in agony as he hung from the horn of the bull by the skin of his arm. To stop this kind of shit happening, to save fools from themselves, there are *los mozos*. Twenty-five of the fittest young lads in the town follow the bulls carrying these long bamboo switches, which they use to beat the living shit out of anyone who tries to touch one of the animals.

The final half hour, the tension is savage. I'm doing my last piece to camera behind the lines of cops that separate the runners from the gates of the bull enclosure. At the high walls overhead, hundreds of spectators are leaning over, waiting. Watching the clock. We head down to the bottom of Calle Estafeta, to the point I'm going to take off from.

'**I'D SEEN PEOPLE TOSSED ON THOSE HORNS LIKE PUPPETS,** SEEN THEM STRETCHED OUT IN HOSPITAL THE FOLLOWING DAY WITH BROKEN LEGS, PUNCTURED RECTUMS, SLASHED STOMACHS, EIGHTEEN-INCH WOUNDS. I'D SEEN THE BLOOD ON THE COBBLES.'

We've fixed a small camera to my shoulder, and I'm going to hold another in my hand. The seconds crawl by. Lads are jumping on the spot, clenching and unclenching their fists. Moving, constantly moving. Seven-fifty-eight, the shout goes up. A roar that builds from the gates back up at Santo Domingo and ripples down through the runners. Everyone cranes their necks to see what's happening . . . Then it comes, the low bang, like a depth charge. **The first firework. El cohete. Three hundred yards away, the gates have opened, and six of the meanest bulls in Spain are tearing down the street towards us. Already the running starts.** Lads are fighting every instinct, trying to hold on, hold on, but as the rush starts, as people start streaming by you, it's almost impossible to resist. You want to wait to see them, you want to wait to actually see the bulls, but now people are pouring past you, picking up speed all the time. The spectators see them before we do, they're pointing and shouting, then you're picked up by the crowd, and that's it. You're gone, you're running. Sprinting. There's roaring behind us, above us . . . In seconds we've covered over ninety yards and I see the barrier, the stretch of high wooden fencing with the Red Cross waiting in behind. This is it, this is where I get off.

I break from the pack, hit the fence and I'm safe. I turn back just in time to see them, all six, still packed tight together, streaming past. The sense of violence, of power. This old guy, dodging out of the way across from me, he falls, smacks his head on the cobbles. Blood. As soon as the coast clears, the Red Cross are out over the fence and across to him.

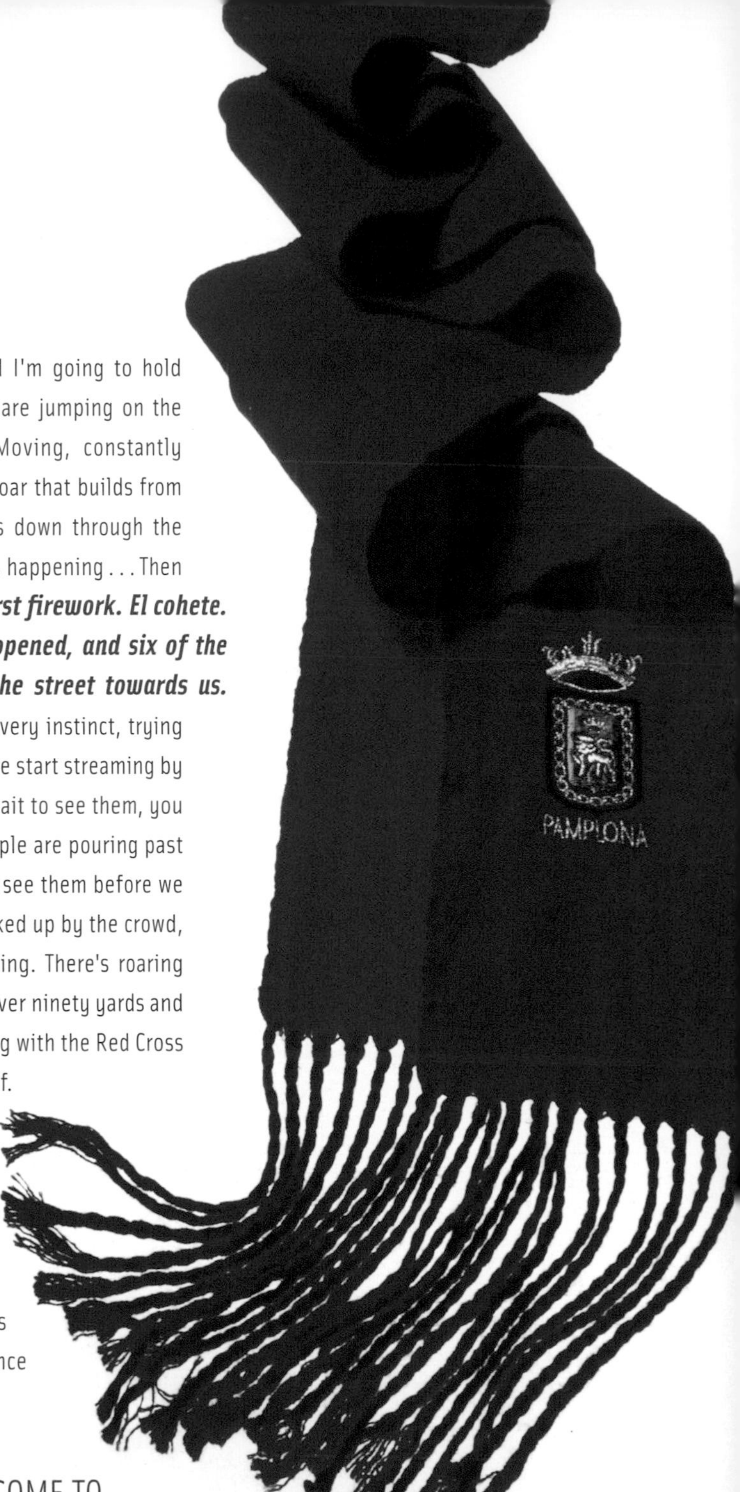

❝IF YOU THINK THE IRISH CAN PARTY, COME TO PAMPLONA FOR THE FIESTAS DE SAN FERMÍN. THESE LADS WILL TEACH YOU WHAT PARTYING IS ALL ABOUT. AND IF THE BULLS DON'T GET YOU, THE ALCOHOL SURE WILL.❞

But the buzz. The sense of relief, of satisfaction at having done it. The runners are milling around, their faces lit up, talking about their experience of it. How close they came. How many fell? How many were trampled? Was anyone gored? We walk back up through the throng. Five minutes earlier you could have cut the air with a knife; now people are laughing, clapping each other on the back. The Ozzies are whooping and high-fiving. Already the bars are open. On Calle Estafeta they're getting stuck into the Kalimotxo again while an ambulance pushes through the crowd towards the small knot of Red Cross people stooped over yet another gobshite bungi glider. Someone cranks up the music, and off it all goes again.

If you think the Irish can party, come to Pamplona for the Fiestas de San Fermín. These lads will teach you what partying is all about. And if the bulls don't get you, the alcohol sure will.

ME AND THE SPANISH

ON THE 16TH OF MAY 1992, GUNS 'N' ROSES PLAYED SLANE. On May 17th, with the ears still ringing and hungover to hell, I left Navan for Bilbao. Got a lift from Navan to Dublin, bus to Rosslare, boat from Rosslare to Le Havre, by rail from Le Havre to Paris. Took a Métro to the Gare d'Austerlitz, got on an overnight train to Irun-Hendaye (the border crossing with Spain) then found a comfortable spot to curl up in my sheepskin jacket and go to sleep. Was prodded awake by a fat, uniformed conductor several hours later. Are we in Irun yet? I asked him. 'Oh no no no no no no no no Missure. Zis is zee last step Missure.' I hauled myself up and looked out the window, not at blue skies and bronzed Spaniards in t-shirts and shorts. Snow. Fir trees. Snow and fir trees. Lapland? No such luck. Lourdes. I rang my mother. Mam, I said, I'm in Lourdes. 'It's a calling! It's a calling!' She says, proving that Irish mothers never really give up hope. 'That's fantastic, what's it like?'

I've no French. I hate French. I hate France.

Turns out all those announcements over the speakers had something to do with the fact that the train split in Bordeaux, with half of it – the wrong half – going on to Irun and the other half going to Lourdes. Two days earlier I was lying on the Hill of Slane with a flagon of Linden Village. Now I was in the snow in Lourdes waiting for a train to get me the hell out of France.

Got to Bilbao eventually, hung around for three weeks, got offered a job, came home, did a TEFL (Teach English as a Foreign Language) course in Leeson Street, came back to the Basque Country and stayed there for nearly four years.

Muy buenos tiempos.

'I SMACKED MY LIPS. *ME ENCANTA POLLA!* – I ADORE CHICKEN! THE CLASS, FOR SOME REASON, FOUND THIS QUITE FUNNY, WHILE LEIRE, FOR SOME REASON, COULD NO LONGER LOOK ME IN THE EYE. AFTERWARDS, AS EVERYBODY FILED OUT, CHUCKLING AWAY TO THEMSELVES, THIS GUY COMES UP TO THE DESK. 'HEY, HECTOR. *POLLO*. *POLL-O* IS CHICKEN. *POLLA*. *POLL-A* IS THIS.' HE MAKES A GESTURE WITH HIS HAND. GREAT. FANTASTIC. **I HAD JUST EXPLAINED TO MY CLASS HOW MUCH I ADORED COCK.**'

Thing is, you can spend your whole life in Spain hanging around with English speakers and never really learn the language. I shared a flat with an English guy called Tim. Tim was a twat. Knew all about rifles and guns, how to make the best bongs and all that kind of shit. When I could stand no more, I put an ad in a local paper. 'Chico Irlandes busca piso en algorta. Llama al número de teléfono . . .' Got loads of offers. The first girl I met, Nines, was a hairdresser from Zamora. Didn't speak a word of English. I shared a flat with her for three years, this despite the fact that the house was haunted, despite the fact that the night I moved in, she and a load of her mates were trying to perform an exorcism. Since I had fuck-all Spanish and they had no English, it took them a while to explain this to me, but they kept using the phrase *fantasma en casa*. *Fantasma*. You didn't need a whole heap of Spanish to figure that one out. They had candles burning, little jars of vinegar and oil in every room, plus a mad looking young one with long black hair was busy making rings of salt in the kitchen.

Feck it. I'd chance the ghost and if it didn't work out, I could always go back to the twat. I went to bed, locked the door and somehow managed to sleep soundly til morning. Three years and I never saw this ghost. But sometimes, Nines would go silent in mid-chat. 'Now.' she'd say. 'Someone's tapping me on the shoulder now.' Other times she'd come in and ask me why I hadn't locked the door the previous night. Of course I locked the door, I'd tell her. There were three big locks and a chain. No, she'd say, it was wide open when I got up for work this morning. The house had a third bedroom that we tried to let out several times but no-one stayed longer than two nights. They'd all wake to see someone standing at the end of the bed.

My first-ever class was a big gang of final-year students. Seventeen and eighteen year olds. There were of course a couple of extremely good looking girls in the mix. Leire was one. At the end of each class, trying to be a little bit cool, I'd say to them OK, because you're learning English and I'm teaching you, I'm going to give you your chance to get your own back. To Get Your Own Back. Phrasal verb, it means to take revenge . . . you speak English to me, you say what's your favourite food then I will repeat what you have said in Spanish. Unai, you first: 'My favourite food is hamburger'. OK that's good. *Me gustan las hambuergesas*. Everyone giggles at my attempt at Spanish. Undaunted, I keep going. OK, Irene: 'My favourite food is salad and chips.' Ah! *Ensalada y patatas fritas*. On we went round the class until we got to Leire. She goes: 'My favourite food is chicken.' And I go ah, *polla!* In the Basque country they do chicken on these big outdoor spits. You get it with sangria, salad, chips, black pudding and chorizo and it's just gorgeous. So I go, in Spanish, ah *polla*, yeah, I love *polla*. I smacked my lips. *Me encanta polla!* – I adore chicken! The class, for some reason, found this quite funny, while Leire, for some reason, could no longer look me in the eye. Afterwards, as everybody filed out, chuckling away to themselves, this guy comes up to the desk. 'Hey, Hector. *Pollo. Poll-o* is chicken. *Polla. Poll-a* is this.' He makes a gesture with his hand. Great. Fantastic. I had just explained to my class how much I adored cock.

I'd work in the morning and in the afternoon I'd watch things like *El Príncipe de Bel Air* and these bizarre game shows featuring young ones in spangly bikinis with giant decks of cards. All without subtitles of course. We put a big wall chart up in the living room and covered it with new words and phrases as I learned them. Nines said to me – she knew I went out a lot on the weekend – Hector, you like to let your hair down on the weekend. *Me gusta soltarme el pelo los fines de semana*. That phrase was pretty much all I knew for a while.

What's your name?

My name is Hector. I like to let my hair down at the weekends.

Where are you from Hector?

Yes, I like to let my hair down at weekends.

Do you have the correct time Hector?

I like to let my hair down at weekends.

After about three years, I'd listen in to women chatting on the metro and understand every word. People, Spanish people, would ask me directions. I got a right kick out of being able to give them. Seven years later, the Spanish was invaluable on the trip to South America. Sorting out all kinds of bureaucratic messes, interviewing the likes of Ibrahim Ferrer in Cuba . . . mainly though just talking to local people everywhere. Without the language, it would have been only half the experience it turned out to be.

BOLIVIA

YOU TAKE A PARCEL OF COCA LEAVES – THREE OR FOUR WILL DO – PUT A LITTLE FLAVOURED ASH AT THE CENTRE AND ROLL THEM ROUND IT. SLOT THE WHOLE LOT UNDER YOUR LIP AND CHEW.

Trying it in the weigh room of the only legal coca market in La Paz, I used too much ash. Bloody thing tasted like coal, and I had to spit it out. Powerful stuff, though. Despite that I had it only seconds in my mouth, within a minute or two, my jaw and one side of my face were completely numb.

Over there, rolling coca leaves is like putting the kettle on. 'Everybody does it,' one guy told me, 'my mother, my sister, my father, my brother.' And they've been doing it for years. When the Spanish conquistadors were here, they encouraged their workers to chew since it made them oblivious to cold, hunger, hardship and pain. It only grows way up in the highest parts of the mountains, where the air is so thin, it's hard for humans to function. But with a few leaves wedged in the gob, you can keep going for days.

The thinness of the air was the first thing that hit us the second we got off the plane. La Paz, the highest capital city in the world, sits two full miles above sea level. By the time we got to the baggage carousel, I was feeling sick in my stomach and I'd a head on me as if I'd drunk six pints of slops the night before. Rosco was puking before he got into the car. Evan lasted 'til dinner, then he had to run for the jacks. A day and a half later we were fully acclimatized, but we steered clear of the drink the whole time we were there. Two beers and you'd be flying. Flying.

Anyway, nobody would have paid any attention to the Bolivians and their leaf rolling if some bright spark hadn't thought it would be a good idea to chemically synthesize the stuff back in the 1880s. The rest is history. La coca's been illegal in the US since 1920, and, of course, US authorities have been trying, with absolutely zero success, to shut the trade down since then. Here in the market, you've literally hundreds of huge bales of the stuff stacked one on top of the other. And it keeps on rolling in; on trucks, on donkeys and especially oul wans' backs. We met one Peig Sayers lookalike who'd hiked two huge bags for seven hours across the hills. Fifty bucks a bag. Tell us this, I said to the guy who ran the market, who buys all this stuff? 'Intermediaries,' he said without so much as a wink. Intermediaries? Jaysus Christ. No doubt these intermediaries had it in LA within a couple of days, and inside a month, it was probably disappearing up schnozzes all over Ireland.

'OVER THERE, ROLLING COCA LEAVES IS LIKE PUTTING THE KETTLE ON. 'EVERYBODY DOES IT,' ONE GUY TOLD ME, 'MY MOTHER, MY SISTER, MY FATHER, MY BROTHER.' AND THEY'VE BEEN DOING IT FOR YEARS.'

Evan had been talking about it for months. He'd been planning it for even longer. 'Evan,' we used to say, 'if you manage to pull this off, we'll stop complaining about the shitty hotels.'

On one of his endless trawls through the internet, he'd come across a story about a fella who'd visited a prison in La Paz. According to this guy, the place was more or less run by the prisoners themselves, and there was one lad in there who actually got people in and gave guided tours.

It all seemed a bit unlikely.

Anyway, from the day we arrived in Bolivia, Evan was on the phone constantly. You'd only pick up fragments of the conversation. 'Yeah...no that's too late...just give me his number...no, that's no good...OK...OK...' Off the phone, he'd say nothing about how these discussions were going. 'I'm working on it,' was all you'd get out of him. Then, a couple of days before we were due to leave, he hung up the phone and turned to me, grinning. 'Hector,' he says, 'you're going to jail.'

At nine a.m. the following morning, the guide dropped us off at the entrance to a park in the centre of town. He wouldn't get any closer. 'Aquí,' he says, pointing across the road at these huge, blank walls running down one side of the plaza. At the main gate, about fifty yards away, I can see guards patrolling. They're holding M16s and wearing body armour.

I've the transmitter for the radio mike taped to the small of my back. Rosco has the camera stripped right down so it'll fit in a canvas bag. Evan has the airgead, the uisce beatha and the toitíní – everything we were told to bring. All I can think of is that film, *Midnight Express*. The lad standing in the bus on the runway, two kilos of drugs taped to his body, while the Turkish cops close in on him...

Freddie was the guy's name. He'd told us that we'd be expected, that there would be nothing to fear from the guards. As soon as we approached the door, I spotted him on the far side. It had to be him. Tall, scrawny, wearing large, wire-framed shades, he perked up the second he saw us, identifying the three Irish guys as easily as we identified the convicted drug dealer. But between us, there were about ten guys with M16s. Ten heavily armed guards and a big fucking metal detector. Oh shite. Never thought of that. I look back at Rosco, who's got the bag slung nonchalantly over his shoulder, like he tries to sneak a camera into a high-security South American prison every day. But the guards, they've been waiting for us. The big lad at the door smiles, winks, nods inside. 'Muy bien, muy bien, no hay problema.' I'm the first through, the thing starts beeping. None of the other guards even look up. 'Pasa, pasa, pasa.' Rosco . . . Evan . . . We're all through. We're inside.

Freddie comes bouncing up. Big, tall, wizened-looking lad, the spit of Louis Theroux. 'Don't worry, don't worry, it's OK. Welcome, my friend.' I've never heard a huskier voice. It's like his tonsils have been burned off with caustic soda. He ushers us away from the main door, round a corner, into this sheltered inner space. Looking around, I realize that it actually looks like – I mean, it's a café? 'Yeah, restaurants, cafés, whatever you want, no problem. We got Cuban restaurants, Chilean, Venezuelan for the boys from there. There's an ice-cream parlour . . . ' Behind me a woman – a woman – is writing out her *menu del dia* on a blackboard.

The prison, Freddie explains, is a city within a city. The governor is nominally in charge, but whatever happens inside the walls is pretty much up to the prisoners themselves. They run everything. 'When I first came to this prison,' says Freddie, 'I had to pay an entrance fee to the population.' You're not assigned quarters, you've got to rent them. If you've the money, you can buy. Freddie, for example, has seven cells that he rents out, ranging from a bare concrete room of two square yards to a three-storey apartment. If you have money, you can build on. In this section, he says, indicating the courtyard above the café, the cheapest place will cost you 150 Bolivian a month. He tells Rosco to aim the camera up at the third floor. All new, he says. A couple of months ago, these cells were all two-storey.

Throughout the tour, Freddie's got five or six boys in constant attendance. Two up ahead in the direction we're going. Another couple behind us. In every open space, two more are watching the approaches. The camera is in and out of the bag all the time.

We're barely out of the café area when one of the lads whistles back to Freddie, who gestures to Rosco to put it away, fast. This little guy rounds the corner. The spit of Richard Dreyfus. Crumpled shirt half in, half out of his chinos. He makes directly for me, sticks out his hand. 'Bienvenido,' he says, 'a mi cárcel.' Welcome to my prison. Off he goes again. 'That,' says Freddie, when your man's out of sight, 'was the boss.' You mean the governor? No, no, the boss. The real boss. He's a prisoner.

You'd think the big cheese would be the biggest, meanest tattoo-covered weightlifting gorilla in there, but no. Brains run the place. That little guy – a lawyer – got caught with two tons of cocaine in La Paz airport several years earlier.

Off we go, down through these narrow little passages, up stairs, out into a bright courtyard with lads playing football on the concrete down below. A whistle from up ahead. Rosco drops the camera into the bag. Three of the meanest-looking hombres you ever saw saunter by. Colombians, says Freddie. You value your life, don't point a camera at those guys. Everything is done with military precision. Knock, wait, whistle, camera up, camera down. Stay put, move…hurry up, slow down…

He takes us into one of the cells, or what was once a cell, now a three-storey apartment. The first floor is just bare concrete, but up a ladder through a trapdoor, there's the kitchen. The woman of the house cooking spaghetti bolognaise on a gas cooker. Two kids sitting at the table doing their homework. Children? Oh, there's about three hundred kids in the place, says Freddie. They head out for school from here in the morning, come back for lunch, then out again in the evening. Mothers often come to prison for a couple of weeks, then head back home again. And at night, street-kids from the neighbourhood queue up to get in. San Pedro is a much safer place to sleep than the streets of La Paz. I get chatting to the little girl. She's eleven years old and wants to be a vet when she grows up. In the corner of the room, over her bed, there are posters of Shakira and Britney Spears.

Anything can be had for money. 'We have women to come in and take care of needs if they need it. For the guys who like guys we have male prostitutes in the facility. If there's guys who like kiddies, we better not find out.' A child abuser who ends up in San Pedro gets placed on a special rehabilitation programme that the prisoners themselves have worked out, Freddie explains. 'We have an old swimming pool where we throw them. They're usually defecated on, urinated on, then, after each one comes out, they're bent over a table and their pants are pulled down. Then they take three hot chilli peppers, cut them in half and they all go up their backside. As each piece

goes in, it's whispered in their ear, if this behaviour takes place inside the prison, they will die. I've been in here four years, I've yet to hear of a rape.'

Four grammes of coke was Freddie's downfall. He got two years in San Pedro for each gramme. 'Somebody ratted me out,' he says, grinning. Harsh as it sounds, things have been worse. Several years earlier, he got caught in New York with five kilos and got five to life. Jail in America was hell compared to this, he says. And his tourist business is actually getting his sentence reduced. 'It started when four friends came over from the States to visit. I showed them around and about a week later I get a call from a bunch of tourists. Hey, Gary told me I could come see you. I said, OK, what do you want to see me about? I managed to get them all inside and I took them around. When they were leaving, I got two dollars here, five dollars here . . . ' After that, word of mouth saw a steady stream of backpackers showing up at the gates of the prison looking to speak to Freddie. In a place like San Pedro, you can't keep something like this quiet for too long. When the governor got to hear of it, he reacted in a typical South American way. Freddie could keep on bringing people in, but he had to hand over the money. Instead, he gets time off for good behaviour. 'I should be going home in a year and three months instead of four years.'

In the downstairs room of his tenant's converted flat we hand over the hundred dollars and the toitíní. But all Freddie cares about is the Johnnie Walker. When he catches sight of the buidéal coming out of Evan's bag, his beady little eyes light up. 'Oh, man!' He grabs it and holds it up to the light like Gollum with the ring, then spins open the top, takes a quick snifter. Three of his boys are standing around, you can hear them licking their lips, but Freddie isn't in the mood to share. He screws the top back on and stuffs the bottle under his shirt.

'OK, guys, OK, we gotta get you out.'

In jig time, we're back at the gates. Freddie's so buzzed up about the fuisce, he gives us all hugs. Hugs for God's sake. With a nod to the gun-toting guards, we slip gently past them and out into bright Bolivian sunshine.

'Jesus,' says I, out of the corner of my mouth, 'that was mad.'

'Mad,' says Evan

'Mad,' says Rosco

I'll never forget the relief getting back into the van. Over dinner that night we kept going back over it. Jesus, I mean we could have been flung into a cell, stripped, raped, robbed and thrown out the back door. We could have been killed.

'Thought ye were gonna make a TV show, boys? Think again.' I imagined us dragged into a cell and strung up alongside sixty other TV crews. Like something out of *The Count of Monte Cristo*. This little old guy with a long beard. 'Yeah, I'm from CNN, been here forty years.'

It was one of the most amazing, maddest, memorable things we'd ever done.

Didn't stop us complaining to Evan about the shitty hotels, though.

> I'LL NEVER FORGET THE RELIEF GETTING BACK INTO THE VAN. OVER DINNER THAT NIGHT WE KEPT GOING BACK OVER IT. **JESUS, I MEAN WE COULD HAVE BEEN FLUNG INTO A CELL, STRIPPED, RAPED, ROBBED AND THROWN OUT THE BACK DOOR. WE COULD HAVE BEEN KILLED.**

NASHVILLE

THE BARREL IS HEAVILY PADDED ON THE INSIDE. They place it on the dirt directly in front of the chute. You're supposed to brace yourself against the sides. You can't see anything, of course. You're just in there, looking up at this little circle of faraway ceiling, listening to the crowd. Waiting for the roar to go up when they let the bull out. The bull: 1,500 pounds of black Texan savagery. He comes tearing down between the bars, sees the barrel and makes straight for it, head down. You could imagine time slowing down, crouched in there, wedging your arms against the sides, waiting for the impact, shitting a brick.

They wanted me inside the barrel. Rónan, the producer, had set it up without telling me, just to see the look on my face.

Hmmmm. I asked Rob to talk me through it. Rob Smets. Five-times world bull-fighting champion. That's bull-fighting, not bull-riding. They sometimes wear clown gear in the arena, but don't call them clowns. They've got the most important job on the night. When the rider is thrown, they get in there and distract the bull, make sure he doesn't take his rage out on the lad who's been on his back. I asked him who had the most dangerous job, riders or fighters? 'They get one of 'em a night,' he says, referring to the bulls. 'I get all of 'em!' That's how it works. There's dozens of bulls, dozens of riders, but there are only two fighters. They're standing there on the dirt when the animal bursts out of the chute, flailing and bucking and trying his living best to get the rider off.

Rob's short and stout and grins wickedly most of the time. There's a glint in the eye that you can't quite trust. He holds himself stiffly, almost as if he can't turn his head, but see him out there with the bulls and he's as agile as they come.

"**HIS NAME IS BLACK MAGIC, AND LADS, HE'S NOT LIKE YOUR TARBH SA MBAILE.** THERE'S NO RING IN THE NOSE, NO HALF-TON CHAIN WEIGHING HIM DOWN. THIS BOY IS A FINELY HONED, HIGHLY TRAINED ATHLETE, ALL FIRED UP AND RARING TO GO. BIG HUMP BELOW HIS NECK, HORNS STICKING OUT A FOOT EITHER SIDE OF HIS HEAD. BLACK, DEAD EYES."

'I've broken my neck twice,' he tells me. 'The bull's front feet and my feet tangled . . . I broke vertebrae C4, C5 and C6. Then I broke my neck again. I was about this far away from the barrel, he hit me, I shot over, hit the barrel with the top of my head like this and I broke C1, which is the one that holds your skull in place . . . '

Hmmmm. Two broken necks. And he's still at it. And I'm looking for advice from him about getting into a barrel which will be rammed by a raging bull.

'You'll be all right,' he grins. 'If I can dodge them on foot out there all day, you can take a little love tap in that barrel.' Love tap? He describes being flung through the air at 100 mph inside a washing machine as a Love tap? 'The most dangerous thing for a barrel-man,' he goes on, 'is with the bull going by and a leg coming down, a foot sticking in there.'

Hmmmmm, again. Show us the bull.

Black as the ace of spades, the bull is pacing back and forth in his pen when we get round to the holding area. His name is Black Magic, and lads, he's not like your tarbh sa mbaile. There's no ring in the nose, no half-ton chain weighing him down.

This boy is a finely honed, highly trained athlete, all fired up and raring to go. Big hump below his neck, horns sticking out a foot either side of his head. Black, dead eyes. Justin leans in towards the gate with the camera, and the bull goes for him. When I get near, it's the same. Head down, he makes a lunge at me through the bars. Rob is chuckling away to himself. 'Look at his tail, he's wagging like a puppy dog!' Puppy dog my arse. I ask him if this bull always carries on like this. He shrugs, admits he doesn't know this particular one. The second that shadow of doubt crosses his face, my mind is made up. There's no way on earth I'm getting into that barrel.

But I do get up on his back. They bring him up to the chute, where he's penned on all four sides, where he can do very little apart from turn his head. Wiley Peterson, one of the tour's up-and-coming riders, shows up to talk me through it.

Do you think these bulls want to hurt you? I ask him, or just want to get you off?

'Some of them wanna hurt you,' says Wiley. He nods down at Black Magic, who's giving us the evil eye. 'He kinda looks like he wants to hurt people.'

Wiley has a gold medallion embossed with a cross fastened to the bull's back. You obviously have a strong faith?

'Oh yeah, I love Jesus,' says Wiley.

With Wiley on one side and Rob on the other, I lower myself slowly on to the bull's back. He doesn't like this one little bit. Hemmed in on all sides by the steel of the gates, with only inches of wiggle room, he's craning the head back, trying to reach me with his horns. Every few seconds he throws himself against the bars, making them rattle. The power, the pent-up aggression . . .

I'm holding on to the braided strap on his back for dear life, then I see that glint in Rob's eye. He's slid down the other side of the enclosure and his hand has wandered dangerously close to the release mechanism on the gate. When I catch him, he grins and draws the hand back again. 'Here now, Rob . . .'

With that going on on one side, it's hard to concentrate on Wiley showing me the 'suicide wrap'. You draw the strap one extra time around your little finger. It's harder then to extricate yourself, so you stay on longer, so you earn more money. The downside is, well, injury. In bull-riding, you're going to get hurt. The best you can hope for is that it's something mild like a broken bone or a concussion, but every time the gate opens, you run the risk of being maimed or killed.

'AFTERWARDS, I MEET UP WITH ROB AGAIN. HE'S BEEN UP CLOSE AND PERSONAL WITH BLACK MAGIC. A LITTLE TOO CLOSE. HIS LATEST INJURY IS A SIX-INCH GASH IN HIS SHIN, WHICH A DOCTOR IS BUSY STITCHING UP. A LOVE TAP? I ASK HIM. ROB CHUCKLES. **'OH YEAH, JUST A LOVE TAP.'**

And the upside? Fame and fortune. Professional bull-riding (PBR) is one of the fastest-growing sports in the US. Tonight, one rider is going to walk away with $50,000. And at the world finals in Las Vegas in October, there's a prize fund of over $3m. There, any rider who stays on for ten seconds gets $1m straight into his hand. Like rock 'n' roll, PBR has its groupies, the Buckle Bunnies, who follow the tour from town to town and hang around outside the arenas, trying to get photographs and autographs. But rock 'n' roll it ain't. It's a family show, and Wiley isn't alone in his love of Jesus. They hold a prayer service every Sunday before the doors open. You've all these tough as befuck cowboys with their heads lowered, their Stetsons held against their chests, eyes closed, lost in prayer.

That night, the show has all the razzmatazz you'd expect. There's flag-waving, pyrotechnics, a lightshow. They've a young one to sing 'The Star Spangled Banner', and the cowboys all make glitzy entrances, throwing shapes and striking poses. All round the outside of the arena, you've stalls weighed down with all the cowboy gear, from the hat to the boots and everything in between. But the bulls are why everyone's here. Eight seconds, that's what you're aiming for. One hand through the strap, the other can't touch the bull. They've this huge clock up on one side, and you can see the hundredths of a second ticking down. Eight seconds might seem like nothing, but it can go on for ever. These enormous beasts kicking up four or five metres behind them, twisting as they do it, these guys tossed around like rag dolls on top of them . . . Our friend Wiley gets to the magic eight, but another guy, Billy Robinson, steals a few fractions of a second more and goes home with the $50,000.

Afterwards, I meet up with Rob again. He's been up close and personal with Black Magic. A little too close. His latest injury is a six-inch gash in his shin, which a doctor is busy stitching up. A love tap? I ask him. Rob chuckles. 'Oh yeah, just a love tap.'

Back in school in St Pat's, if you saw a pair of
Wranglers on someone, you'd know straight away they were
in on the bus from the arse end of Curragha or Kilskyre. Levis for the
urban sophisticates of Navan, Wranglers for the mucksavages. But in Nashville,
Levis are the wrong trousers. It's Wrangler jeans, the check shirt, the Resistol hat and the
boots. This is the uniform, and anything else is for city slickers.

So we took a walk down Broadway, the main shopping street, to get me kitted out. The first place we went into, we got a crash course in the cowboy lifestyle. The sales assistant was this short, plump cowgal in her mid-forties with about five teeth missing, the rest stumpy and discoloured and a big brown feather sticking out of her Stetson. 'My son shot a turkey for that.' She had a little tin of Copenhagen tobacco, about the same size and shape as a tin of shoe polish. Opened it up, took out a pinch and wedged it behind her bottom lip, just under her teeth. Dipping, she called it. 'I bin dippin' since I was eight years old.' She pulled back her lip to show me. This black mess pasted to her gum. Foul. But shag it, I said I'd have a go. Scooped up a little on my finger, in behind the lip . . . the second I got the taste of the stuff – minty, hot, vile, pukey – I had to tear outside and spit it up. The shit was so strong, I started seeing stars. Jesus, I said to her, how long do you keep that stuff in there? 'Oh, I don't spit it out,' she said. 'I swallow it!' There was this one time, she said, when a cowboy 'laid one on her' and scooped out her tobacco with his tongue and settled it in his own mouth. Shudder.

You like cowboys? I asked her. 'Like 'em? I am one. My last ride was a thirty-two-hundred-pound bull.'

Back in the arena, Joe Lucia, the production manager, reckons the boots and the Stetson make me look like the real deal. The previous day I had bent over to show him my skinny, Levi-clad arse, and this made him really uncomfortable. 'That's one thing cowboys ain't interested in,' he says, with this forced laughter, looking around to see if anyone's watching. Now I tell him I still couldn't bring myself to change to Wranglers and I turn the arse to him again. He holds up his hands and backs away. 'You gotta quit showin' me that,' he says, in a fierce whisper.

Heh heh heh.

NOTTINGHAM

EIGHT OUT OF TEN PEOPLE PUKE. That's what they told me, first thing. Jeremy Clarkson famously redecorated the cockpit of an F15 when he was a passenger. What happens, they said, is that the brain just can't take it. Hurtling through the sky, upside down, at 500 mph. You get hot and sweaty and shaky and you lose your lunch.

Great. Fantastic. Now they tell me, now that it's too late to pull out.

The Red Arrows boys aren't what you'd expect, or not all of them anyway. You've a lot of thinning hair and a fair few pudgy bellies. It's not all chiselled jaws and tally-ho accents either. Sitting in the briefing room the first morning, they spent most of the time talking about golf outings and fancy dress parties. They number themselves. Spike, who's the squadron leader, is Red 1, then it's Red 2, 3, 4, all the way down to the doctor and the engineers at Red 13 and 14. Everything is synchronized. The day starts with a weather briefing on the dot of eight-forty. Spike counts it down. 'Met report in ten, nine, eight . . . ' and so on. Then the rest of the day, it's the same thing.

'Everybody, watches please . . . Counting down to nine-fifteen in ten, nine, eight . . . zero. Cup of tea anyone?'

'Counting down to twenty-thirty in ten, nine, eight . . . zero. Few scoops, lads?'

All they do is train, day in, day out. Loops and rolls, loops and rolls. Practising endlessly until the manoeuvres are perfect. 'We select people very carefully,' says Spike, 'and we select very talented aviators. We then train them very hard and we push them into areas that perhaps they've never even considered before.' It might be hard work, but the perks are pretty damn good. These lads are the public face of the RAF. While they might spend all their time training in Nottingham, every couple of months, there'll be a major airshow somewhere in the world, and the Red Arrows will be there. And of course it's a shit cool job. In the car park of the base,

'THE RED ARROWS BOYS AREN'T WHAT YOU'D EXPECT, OR NOT ALL OF THEM ANYWAY. YOU'VE A LOT OF THINNING HAIR AND A FAIR FEW PUDGY BELLIES. **IT'S NOT ALL CHISELLED JAWS AND TALLY-HO ACCENTS EITHER.** SITTING IN THE BRIEFING ROOM THE FIRST MORNING, THEY SPENT MOST OF THE TIME TALKING ABOUT GOLF OUTINGS AND FANCY DRESS PARTIES.'

' WE'RE HERE FOR THREE DAYS, WITH MY FLIGHT SCHEDULED
TO TAKE PLACE ON THE THIRD DAY. IN THAT TIME, IT GETS PRETTY
CLEAR THAT, EVEN THOUGH PUKING ISN'T THE ONLY THING I HAVE
TO WORRY ABOUT, **PUKING IS THE ONE THING ON EVERYBODY'S MIND.** '

you've top-of-the-line Sierra Cosworths, BMW M5s, Audi TTs. For the younger lads, the ones who aren't married, you can be sure that being a Red Arrow goes down well in Blazers in Nottingham on a Saturday night.

We're here for three days, with my flight scheduled to take place on the third day. In that time, it gets pretty clear that, even though puking isn't the only thing I have to worry about, puking is the one thing on everybody's mind. Dave is the scrimper, the guy in charge of fixing me up with the uniform and all the safety gear. As he potters around with his measuring tape, I ask him if he's ever gone up for a spin. No, he says. 'I've been offered it, don't get me wrong, it's just that when I feel a bit braver, I'll take the bull by the horns.'

This doesn't exactly fill me with confidence. I've said it before and I'll say it again, this isn't teilifís le haghaidh na jackasses. You can have your roller-coasters, your walls of death and your paraskiboardbasewheeling. I'd rather have the cupán tae.

Dave takes a couple of folded white bags and slots them into these little pouches just above the bottoms of the trousers. 'Pick and mix bags,' he calls them. It takes me a second to realize that he's being funny. There's a couple in a pocket in the cockpit, he says, but these ones in the trousers are for easy access if we're upside down when the breakfast wants to come back up.

Besides the helmet and the visor, there's this double face-mask – for oxygen and communications – which is crammed tight against your face and screwed in with little bolts on the sides. Getting these off in a hurry will not be easy. 'If you do have to blow chunks,' says Dave, 'put the radio into the off position, take the mask away from your face and then you can get your pick and mix out and use that.' Yeah, right. Easier said than done.

At the medical, the guy tells me not to have any breakfast on the day of the flight. Puke. It's all anyone can talk about.

But the real fun starts that morning. I meet Steve Underwood, my pilot. For forty minutes, I'll be putting my life in his hands. He's a big, solid, dependable-looking chap, but one of the first things he says throws me off balance again.

'We'll let you have a go.'

'You'll what?'

'We'll let you have a go.'

'To fly the aircraft?'

'You're going to roll it and loop it.'

'I am, yeah.'

'Yes you are . . . I'm a fully qualified flying instructor, I won't let you kill me, I won't let you damage the aircraft, but you are definitely going to loop it and roll it.'

'How am I going to do that?'

'I'm going to show you.'

The closest I've ever come to rolling a Red Arrows Hawk was hitting a pothole on the bog road from Navan to Athboy in my Fiat Punto 1.2sx one time.

In the training room, they've set up a seat identical to the one in the plane. Steve takes me through the procedures and talks about everything that's going to happen once we're in the air. G force is the big deal. As the jet approaches its top speed of around 500 mph, a force equal to five times gravity is exerted on the body. This means that there are times during the flight when you weigh five times what you do on the ground. To deal with it, you've a body suit that you plug into the console under the seat. During the flight, this fills with air and stops you from rattling around inside the cockpit. It's still rough as fuck on the body, though, and there's every possibility I might pass out.

Steve tells me that once we hit G3, I'm to start groaning and keep groaning until we're out the other side of it. Groaning? Why do I have to groan? Why not just keep talking to him? Because, he says, at G5, groaning is the only thing I'll be able to do.

Right. Great.

Then we get to the safety belt. 'When you put the straps in, put them to either side of your testicles because if you're pulling four or five G and they're caught in the strap you'll know all about it.'

Ouch. The thought of it makes my eyes water. Sobering as all as this is, what he says next makes me forget about liathróidí, puke and everything.

'If I think we have to leave the aircraft,' he says, 'I'll say, "Hector, things aren't looking too good in here, we'll have to step over the side very shortly. I can't eject you. It's your life in your hands with that handle." I will say, "Eject, eject, eject."' The handle he's referring to is the big yellow one under the seat. The one that says Do Not Pull. You grab it and you pull with all your might. There's something like 40 lbs of explosive underneath the seat and that handle detonates it. Two seconds after you engage it, you're a hundred metres from the plane.

After this, I can't help but think of all that amateur footage you see of planes careering into the crowd at airshows. The evening news is playing in my head. 'Tragedy struck at Scrampton air base this afternoon during a routine training mission . . . ' This was the fifty-sixth Amú show, the last one ever. I think it's safe to say that I did not want to go out in a blaze of glory.

The worst point comes after they strap me in. The belt is so tight, I can hardly move. Besides the helmet and the visor, there are the twin masks clamped in tight against my face, the oxygen pipe sticking in my mouth like that suction thing the dentist uses. It's sweaty and claustrophobic, and the cockpit reeks of petrol. Outside the window, I watch the other planes lining up on either side of us. I wriggle around the seat, making sure, for the fortieth time, that the liathróidí aren't in the way of the straps.

I'm not happy.

But every scrap of discomfort and nervousness evaporates as soon as we start moving. The coordination is just amazing. All nine planes move off at the exact same moment and remain perfectly aligned as we accelerate down the runway. All take to the air as if they were one unit, and the take-off is so smooth, you'd hardly know you'd left the ground. Within seconds of leaving the tarmac, we've broken up through the grey, drizzly skies above Lincoln and are rising into the clear blue air above the cloudline. Wing to wing, barely four feet between each plane. It's a beautiful sight. 'How are you doing, Hector?' Steve's voice comes over the radio. He's easing me in gently. 'Are you ready to try something?' I give him the thumbs up and off we go. Breaking ranks with the others, the ascent gets steeper and steeper until we're heading straight up, at ninety degrees to the ground. Back at base, Steve had coached me on this bit. 'Keep your head turned back, keep your eyes on the horizon. You have to focus your mind on the ground because your brain won't like what

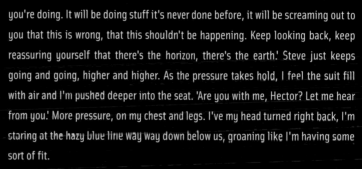

LATER THAT YEAR, THE RED ARROWS WERE IN GALWAY FOR THE AIRSHOW AND I MET THEM ALL DOWN IN THE RADISSON THE NIGHT OF THE PERFORMANCE. **IT WAS THE NIGHT MY SON RÍAN WAS BORN.** BEFORE I HEADED BACK UP TO THE HOSPITAL, I SET THEM ALL UP WITH BABY GUINNESSES AND SENT THE YOUNGER LADS DOWN TO CPS TO CHECK OUT THE LOCAL TALENT.

you're doing. It will be doing stuff it's never done before, it will be screaming out to you that this is wrong, that this shouldn't be happening. Keep looking back, keep reassuring yourself that there's the horizon, there's the earth.' Steve just keeps going and going, higher and higher. As the pressure takes hold, I feel the suit fill with air and I'm pushed deeper into the seat. 'Are you with me, Hector? Let me hear from you.' More pressure, on my chest and legs. I've my head turned right back, I'm staring at the hazy blue line way way down below us, groaning like I'm having some sort of fit.

Eventually, the plane tops out. 'OK, Hector, I want you to take that stick in front of you, push it all the way to the right and hold it there.'

Oh shit, here goes. I reach out tentatively and grab the smooth rubber handle. One, two, three. I sweep it over to the right. The plane flips over, once . . . twice. It's an amazing feeling, to be in control of the plane, to make it spin like that.

But I'm only getting into it when the whole thing is over.

Back on the ground, two things happen. First, the air hisses out of the pressure suit and I suddenly feel as though I've played a full game of football in hot sunshine. Completely knackered. This is OK, I can deal with this, but next minute, I get the crappiest, queasiest feeling I've ever had. Shaky and sweaty and certain that whatever I'd eaten the previous day is on its way back up. Steve, I say, I'm going to puke. 'Don't worry, you're fine, you're going to be fine, just let it pass, it's your body returning to normal, it happens all the time, you're not going to be sick. It'll pass.' It passes. A minute later I am fine again. Back out on the tarmac, Steve presents me with the empty puke bags and says to keep them as a trophy. Great. No puke, and no ejector seat either. I thought I might have to do the closing piece to camera dangling by a parachute from a tree somewhere.

Later that year, the Red Arrows were in Galway for the airshow and I met them all down in the Radisson the night of the performance. It was the night my son Rían was born. Before I headed back up to the hospital, I set them all up with Baby Guinnesses and sent the younger lads down to CPs to check out the local talent.

A CAUTIONARY TALE II

YOU FLY IN, YOU GET A DAY TO ACCLIMATIZE AND THEN YOU START SHOOTING. WE NEVER DRINK THE DAY BEFORE WORK. WELL, ALMOST NEVER. In Nashville, we took a stroll through town on the first morning to take in the atmosphere. It's Galway sized, the home of the cowboy, with music everywhere you turn. Buskers on every corner – good ones too – beating out the country standards. This warm, relaxed, southern feel to it. John Deere is king. Every shop you go into has John Deere belt buckles, jump suits, jigsaws, fridge magnets.

Then I spotted the bar. A huge sports bar with massive plasma screen TVs, cowboys propping up the counter and about twenty pool tables. Not just any pool tables either, but pool tables with different colour baize! Not just green! I love that. Luminous pink, turquoise, aquamarine . . . All the colours of the rainbow, each with one of those low lights hanging over it. You could hear the click of the balls with the country and western playing constantly in the background. Class.

Eight hours later, we staggered out. Cocktails and tequila slammers, challenge games with the locals. Coors Light and Bud Light, that's all they drink. Every time you were halfway through your bottle, another ice bucket would appear with three longnecks sticking out of it. Cowboy heaven.

I woke up with that familiar throbbing just behind the left temple. Realized I'd left the Solpadeine at home. Fuck. Then the horrible truth dawns. Obair. We have to go to work. Ah fuck. The people from the PBR were expecting us at seven a.m. So, in the scorching heat of the Nashville morning, we piled into a taxi with all the gear, but got out at the wrong place, so had to haul cameras, batteries, lights, tripods, all that shit half a mile around to the right place, only to be told, no lads, you've to go back to the main entrance about a half a mile back the way we came. Fuck this. There are few things worse than a bad hangover in intense heat. I don't care how late we're going to be, I need coffee, I need drugs and some kind of fizzy drink. Still laden down with all Justin's camera gear, we struck out for a shop up on the top of a hill. Wal-Mart. I'd never been in a Wal-Mart before. Tylenol. Extra Strength Codeine. Oh yes. I bought about six packets. Tylenol for period pains. Four of those, thanks very much. Next, liquids. Four different colour Gatorades, one to match the colour of each of the pool tables we'd played on the night before. Then across the road to Starbucks. Big bucket of iced Frappuccino. Things were starting to improve.

Back down in the arena, no one was bothered by the fact that we were about three hours late. In a real stroke of luck, Justin ran into serious problems with the microphones and I found a cosy little back room to curl up with my period pain Tylenol and catch a couple of hours sleep while he sorted it out. Nothing like technical hitches when you've a hangover.

FLESH

GOING WHERE THE STREETS HAVE NO SHAME. BOYS WHO LIKE GIRLS WHO LIKE BOYS WHO LIKE GIRLBOYS WHO LIKE PIRATED COPIES OF TAKE THAT CDS & HAVE HUGE HAIRY KNUCKLES

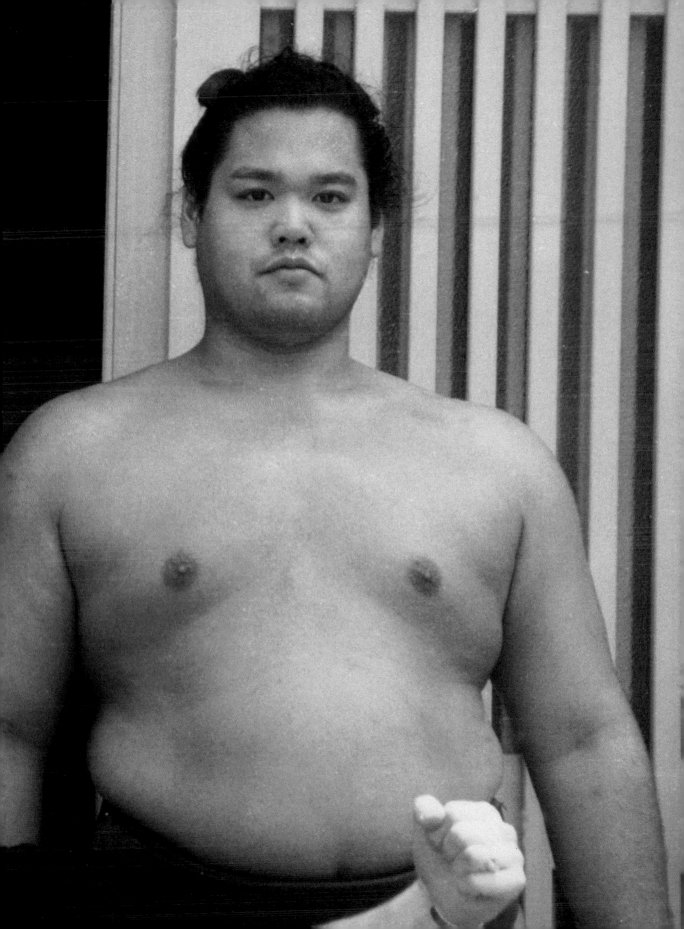

AMSTERDAM

>*PROSTITUTE:* **Hey, baby!** *You come inside,* **we fuck?**

>**HECTOR:** Dia Dhuit.

>*PROSTITUTE:* Ah…*Sprechen Sie* **Deutsch?**

>**HECTOR:** NÍ HEA. GAEILGE.

>*PROSTITUTE:* **Español?** *Parlez-vous français?*

>**HECTOR:** **Níl, níl.** Conas atá do chuid Gaeilge?

>*PROSTITUTE:* ITALIANO?

>**HECTOR:** NÍL, NÍL, NÍL – *cé mhéad le haghaidh post gaoth?*

>*PROSTITUTE:* **You are Danish?**

>**HECTOR:** NÍ HEA. Is Éireanach me, is breá liom prataí agus tá bata mór ramhar agam. Anois, cé mhéad le haghaidh gnéas.

>*PROSTITUTE:* *Sex?* **You wanna fuck?**

>**HECTOR:** GNÉAS. CÉ MHÉAD LE HAGHAIDH GNÉAS?

'BUT IT WAS ALSO A SCARY SHOW TO MAKE.
THE RED-LIGHT DISTRICT. AN SOLAS DEARG.
IT MIGHT SEEM LIKE NO MORE THAN
A WEIRD KIND OF TOURIST ATTRACTION, BUT
THERE'S THIS NASTY LITTLE UNDERCURRENT
ALWAYS BUBBLING UNDER. THE COPS DON'T
GO DOWN THERE.**'**

That word Gnéas. Gnnnnnéas. It might be the first time anyone ever spoke Irish to her, but she got that word. It just sounds dirty, or at least it does if you use the right tone of voice.

The Amsterdam show was a landmark one for us. The last programme in the second series, we managed to get away with stuff that you shouldn't really get away with at eight o'clock on a Sunday evening. Besides going sex shopping in the red-light district, we found a guy who'd smoke dope on camera. Amazing what you can get away with if you do it through Irish.

But it was also a scary show to make. The red-light district. An solas dearg. It might seem like no more than a weird kind of tourist attraction, but there's this nasty little undercurrent always bubbling under. The cops don't go down there. We went to see them the day we were going to take the cameras in - you need to get a licence to film in most of these places - and they refused to grant one. Don't go down there, they said. If you do, we won't protect you. It's controlled by the pimps and the brothels. If you get caught in there with a camera, well. The cop shrugged, as if to say, if you wind up floating face down in the canal, don't come running to us.

So we thought about it for a while and decided, fuck it, it'd be worth a lash. We went down to the supermarket and bought a black shoulder-bag. Back at the hotel, Barry the cameraman cut a hole in it, stripped down the camera and fitted it inside, heavily padded so it wouldn't move. He tried a few manoeuvres while we watched, angling it here and there, hitting the record button without seeming to. You could just about make out the shine of a black lens sticking out of the hole, but you'd have to be damn sharp to realize what it was. While the boys put the finishing touches to the camera, I did a mafia job on the radio mike. Concealed it inside my shirt with the little radio pack at my back just inside the belt.

The red-light district itself has this Ilac Centre feel to it, except of course instead of clothes and cafés and electronic goods, it's women in fluorescent underpants. We got down there about ten, just as the crowds were thickening up. During the day, you'll get families wandering around, but at night, it's packs of Italians and half-scuttered English stag parties. Business was brisk.

Things started badly. Everyone's on the move, going from one window to the next, staring up as long as they can get away with it before shuffling on to the one beside it. The second we slowed down and began scouting for a good place to start filming, we stuck out like three sore mickeys. These lads materialized out of nowhere. 'Hey you! You fuck off!' It was like they knew exactly what we were about. Off again, trying to look a bit cooler. Down the strip, into the throng, down through these weird little alleys with those lurid red and purple lights, the bored-looking women posing and pouting in their windows. Here and there a closed curtain with business going on behind it. I'm about halfway down, walking ahead of the two boys, when this beast of a woman – she must have weighed about eighteen stone – leans out of her doorway and starts calling out to me. 'Hey! Come on in here, come on in!'

I slowed down to talk to her and she swooped. Grabbed me, pulled me in, drew over the curtain, locked the fucking door! It was like being gobbled by a whale. All right, all right, I'm a professional. I'm there trying to make the best of it, get something decent on the mike. I start asking her prices. Seventy for sex, she says, fifty for a blowjob. That's grand, that's grand, says I, moving towards the door. Ceart go leor, I'll go talk to me mates. But she blocks the way. 'No no. We fuck now, we fuck now,' her big, pudgy hands get busy, she grabs my belt and starts at the buckle. No, no, I go talk to my friends. All I can think of is the mike. If she finds the mike, she'll start screaming, and there'll be about fifteen Huggy Bears in on top of us. She mistakes my reluctance for bargaining and the price drops. 'It's just fifty, everything fifty. Wanna fuck now?'

I wanna get the fuck out of there, and fast. I'm looking at the inner door, half expecting the heavies to come pouring in: 'What's the problem? What's the problem here?' Five minutes, I'm thinking, I'll be over the back of someone's sofa with an apple wedged in my mouth. Some guy opening a tub of Vaseline. 'OK, Irish boy . . .'

Red-

Dis

THE RED-LIGHT DISTRICT ITSELF HAS THIS ILAC CENTRE FEEL
TO IT, EXCEPT OF COURSE INSTEAD OF CLOTHES AND CAFÉS AND
ELECTRONIC GOODS, IT'S WOMEN IN FLUORESCENT UNDERPANTS.

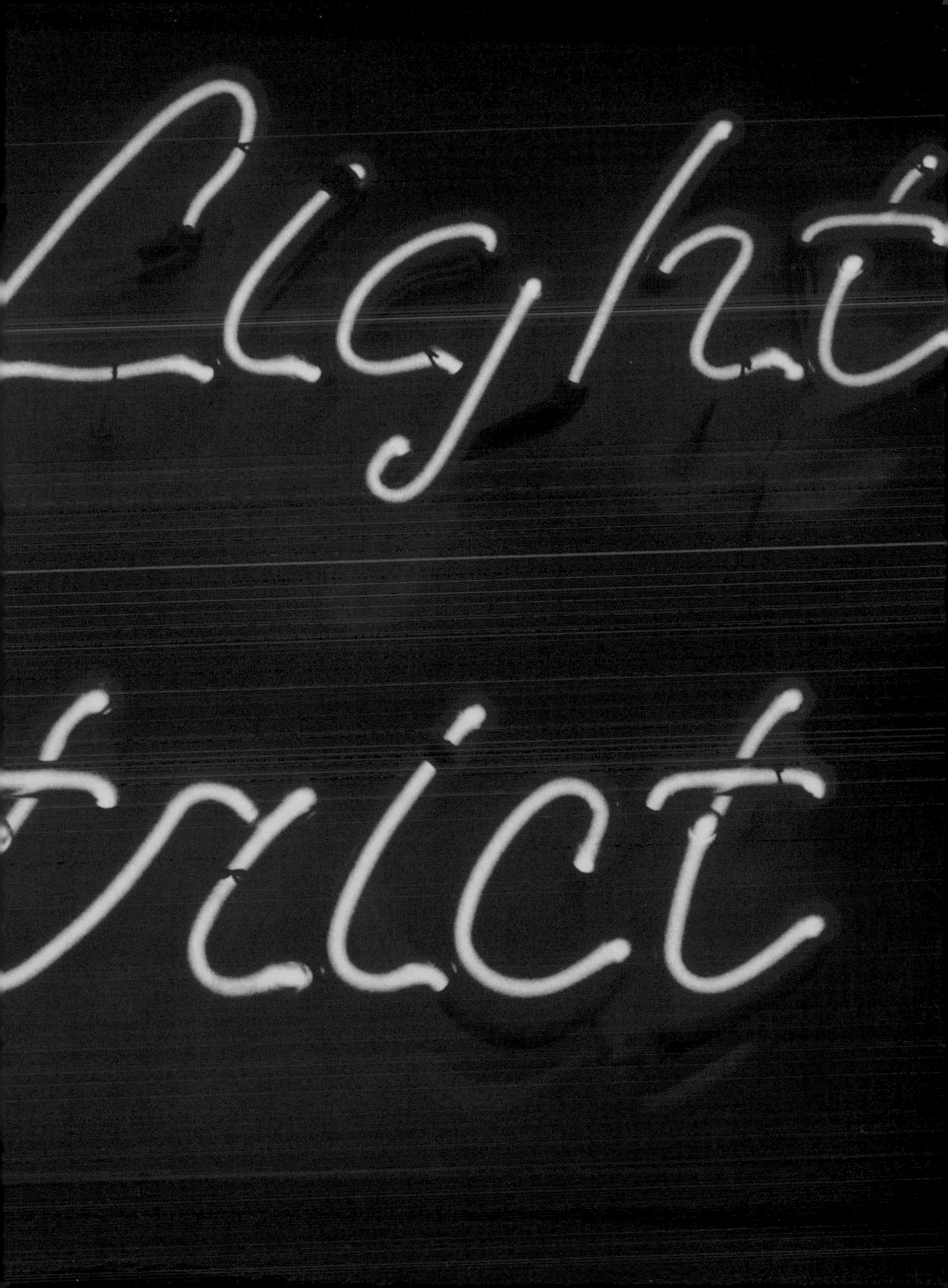

A couple of years earlier, I'd been in Amsterdam with about a dozen of my mates. As we were coming back through the red-light area at three in the morning, this car screeched to a halt in front of us and these Middle Eastern dudes climbed out, about four of them. They'd got guns. They were waving them in front of our faces, shouting stuff at us in Dutch. We thought we were fucked. We, each of us, thought we were going to get shot. I've no idea what they were looking for, but after a few seconds, they put the guns away and got back in the car. You forget that, *besides all the coffee houses and girls in windows, there's this hardcore side to Amsterdam. Class A drugs, smuggling, mafia. The Altar Boy, the Viper, the Five Bar Gate, the Food Processor, the Bin Liner - all those lunatics, they're all here.*

So anyway, this sperm whale is there, grabbing at my bits, and I'm trying to edge round her like a frightened sheep. She gets distracted, loses heart or something, I dart round, get the door open and make a bolt for freedom.

After that, there's no more boxing above my weight. I stick close to the two boys and give the big mommas a wide berth.

But the aim the whole time is to deal as Gaeilge, something that's bloody hard to pull off when you get right down to it. These girls, they're wide to everything. Trading sex has always been legal here, but it wasn't until 1999 that the government brought in legislation to make the brothels legal too. Why? Because the prostitutes' union, The Red Thread, campaigned for it. Keep it in the open, keep it safe. There's even a Prostitutes' Information Centre - which is a designated charitable organization. They run courses in prostitution, they run language classes; there's fuck all that these girls haven't heard before. The minute I say 'Dia Dhuit', she hears the gutteral Dh and she thinks, German, he's German. I'm sticking rigidly to the Irish, trying to make out I don't understand a word, but it's like that game you used to play in school where you had to answer twenty questions without saying yes or no. You can't even nod, you can't give any indication you know what she's saying.

'You want sex?'

'Céard? Ni thuigim. Cé mhéad le haghaidh bualadh leathar?'

'Ah tá Gaeilge agat! Maith go leor a mhac. Bain síos na brísti go tapaidh and luigh síos ar an leaba. Fan nóiméad agus cuirfidh me píosa ceoil ar súil. An maith leat Seoirse Michael?'

Did you ever take a pull out of that oul joint, Hector? It's a question I get asked all the time.

You couldn't go to Amsterdam without covering the dope. Or you could, but what would be the point? I mean, everyone who goes to Amsterdam from Ireland, yeah there's the architecture and the cuisine and the art and the folk dancing, there's Van Gogh and Anne Frank, but really, in all fairness, it's about the sex and the drugs. Boners and stoners. It's the coffee houses and the dope. The Lebanese Gold, the Afghan Black, the Northern Lights. The B52, Purple Haze and the White Widow. The widow is always white.

Everywhere we went during the first two series, we looked for interesting people who'd talk Irish on camera. In Amsterdam, we wanted to take it a bit further and find someone who'd be prepared to smoke as Gaeilge. Someone who'd get clocháilte. Nollaig Mac Sheoin, a year and a half in the place, was just such a man. He was working in a bar over there, taking a break from his degree. A long, long break.

He took me round through the best coffee houses in town. It was a peculiar experience. For a start, Nollaig's Irish got steadily worse with each stop we made. And for some reason our progress slowed right down. At one point we were nearly run over by two cops on horseback. You'd think we'd be slightly shaken by an experience like that, but, for some reason, we found it hilarious. Very odd.

Next thing we knew, we were both ravenously hungry, but Nollaig knew what to do. He took me to Febo, this specialist fast-food place located within easy reach of most of the coffee houses. Here, instead of your usual fast-food format, you've dozens of little glass boxes. Inside each, there are individual portions: a cheese sandwich, a burger, a kebab, a bag of chips. You just pop the coins through the slot, the little door opens and you grab your snack. You don't have to talk to anybody. It's very handy for people who, for no reason at all, suddenly become incapable of making sense.

Anyway, we ended up in this pub, and your man shakily skinning up another big fat spliff. I took it off him, but would I take a pull out of the thing on camera? Would I fuck.

It was the last show of the second series. We didn't know if there'd be a third. Sitting in this pub in Amsterdam, waving a joint in the camera, I asked anyone who'd like to see us in Asia, Africa or wherever to cuir glaoch ar TG4. Inside a couple of minutes, the phonelines were jammed, and a few months later, we were off again. Class.

IT WAS THE LAST SHOW OF THE SECOND SERIES. WE DIDN'T KNOW IF THERE'D BE A THIRD. SITTING IN THIS PUB IN AMSTERDAM, WAVING A JOINT IN THE CAMERA, I ASKED ANYONE WHO'D LIKE TO SEE US IN ASIA, AFRICA OR WHEREVER TO CUIR GLAOCH AR TG4. INSIDE A COUPLE OF MINUTES, THE PHONELINES WERE JAMMED, AND A FEW MONTHS LATER, WE WERE OFF AGAIN. CLASS

The John and Yoko Suite

The nice people in the Amsterdam Hilton showed us up to the room where John and Yoko took to the bed for a week in 1969. They gave us the keys and left us at it. Maybe because they were laid-back Dutch people, maybe I do a better impression of a responsible adult than I think I do. Everything was exactly the same, right down to the graffiti on the window: **HAIR PEACE BED PEACE**. All round the walls, there are photos of the pair of them surrounded by news crews, gurus, monks, journalists and photographers. If it wasn't for the fact that Yoko came back and gave the place a makeover ten years ago, it would be as if they'd just got out of bed and walked out of the room.

Anyway. I don't know what it is about a 'Do Not Touch' sign. Five minutes after the hotel people left, I was sitting up in the bed with the togs off, playing the opening riff from 'Sunday Bloody Sunday' on John Lennon's guitar. It's the only thing I know. Sure, if they'd really expected us to leave it alone, they'd have screwed it into the wall, or at least they'd have screwed it a whole lot tighter into the wall.

WON'T

Teach You in Coláiste na bhFiann
(Not in the Classrooms Anyway)

>*BLOWJOB*   *n.* post gaoth

>*CONDOM*   *n.* **coiscín**

>*ERECT PENIS*   *n.* bod in a sheasamh

>*MAD*   *a.* imithe, **as an bosca**

>*MASTURBATION*   *v.* **féin truailliú** (LIT. SELF POLLUTION)

>*PENIS*   *n.* bod, michilín, seán tomás, bata, slat, **nathair nimhe**

>*PROSTITUTE*   *n.* striopach, cailín sráide

>*SCROTUM*   *n.* **do mhála**

>*SEX*   *n.* gnéas, *v.* **bualadh leathar** (LIT. SLAPPING LEATHER)

>*SHIT*   *n.* cac; *to have a shit,* na páistí a fhágáil ag an linnsnamh;
                    I had a shit, d'fhág mé na páistí ag on linnsnamh;
                    I don't give a shit, **Is cuma sa cac.**

>*STONED*   *a.* clocháilte

>*TESTES*   *n.* **liathróidí,** magairle (NOT TO BE CONFUSED WITH MAGERLY'S
                    PIE, A DELICACY UNIQUE TO E210'S CHIPPER IN NAVAN)

>*VAGINA*   *n.* Gabhal, bosca, **puisín**

BANGKOK

I'LL BET IT HAPPENS ALL THE TIME. Young Tommy, in second-year engineering in Dundalk IT, is on his way over to Australia for the year and he stops off in Bangkok for a couple of nights with all his mates. Bangkok, the Vegas of Asia. He's heard all the stories. The beer, the dope, the strange pills. Pat Pong. The live shows. Ping-pong balls and cigars. Up to this point, Tommy's sexual education hasn't progressed beyond the odd lucky grope in the back seat of his brother's Honda Civic in the car park of the Oasis Niteclub in Carrickmacross. He's not expecting too much of his 48-hour stopover in Bangkok, but sure, he'll have a look around, take in all the sights, maybe have a few stories to tell when he gets to Oz.

The city's an assault on the senses. It's loud, noisy, smelly and brightly lit all the time. The streets are packed with stalls, the bars never close. Along the strip in Pat Pong, the neon signs are blinking and fizzing, there's girls hanging out of windows, singing out to Tommy to come in and have a look. After a few hours, a dozen Tiger beers and maybe a few local chemicals, he's sitting cross-eyed in the latest bar. 'Sussudio' by Phil Collins is blaring from the speakers. Suddenly, across the room, he notices this raven-haired beauty staring directly at him. As their eyes meet, she smiles coyly and bats her inch-and-a-half eyelashes. Can it be? Long, straight locks of lustrous black hair, olive skin, perfect teeth . . . Is this oriental Andrea Corr really making eyes at him? Me? Says Tommy, pointing at himself. She beams and nods. Sweet divine mother of Jesus, thinks Tommy, there is a God. She gets to her feet and slinks over to where he sits in a widening pool of sweat. The figure-hugging dress confirms that the body is everything the face promised it would be.

The rest is a blur. There's snuggling and giggling, several more Tiger beers, maybe

FERTILITY SHRINE

> **BANGKOK, THE VEGAS OF ASIA.**
> HE'S HEARD ALL THE STORIES.
> THE BEER, THE DOPE, THE
> STRANGE PILLS. PAT PONG.
> THE LIVE SHOWS. PING-PONG
> BALLS AND CIGARS.

a few more dodgy chemicals. Somehow he gets separated from his mates and finds himself in some darkened back room, where he's becoming ever-more familiar with the bould Andrea. There's slurping and pawing and encouraging moans from herself. But eventually it comes, that dreadful moment. Titeann lámh Tommy síos í dtreo an gleann only to discover that Andrea isn't all she's cracked up to be.

Andrea is in fact Andrew.

You may say you'd never get caught, boys, but remember that scene in *The Crying Game*. These lads can fool the lad. Beware! If you ever find yourself in Bangkok, hitting it off with a young one who wouldn't be seen dead with you at home, chances are it is too good to be true. Two things. Check the throat and the backs of the hands. There's no hiding the Adam's apple or the large knuckles on the buachaill cailíní of Bangkok

There are four million ladyboys in Thailand. In a population of twenty million, that's a whole heap of sexual confusion. There are three basic types:

The home bird. Totally accepted and integrated into Thai society, this she-lad is quite content to spend his life at the mammy's side, cooking the green curry for the da, washing his sisters' hair and listening to pirated copies of Take That CDs. He'll end up in old age watching Thai soap operas and dubbed reruns of *Dynasty* and *Falcon Crest*.

The entertainer. He leaves the closet in splinters in his race to get out, leave the family in the mountains and take to the stage down in Bangkok. Knows every Abba song ever written and has made up dance routines for most. Is only happy in ostrich feathers, thick make-up and weighed down by half a ton of sequins.

The professional. Think of Catherine Zeta Jones, except with a penis. Dark, sultry, stunningly beautiful. Plies the main tourist drag, tossing the head and flashing ample lengths of carefully shorn thigh. Will perform various forms of sexual favour if the price is right.

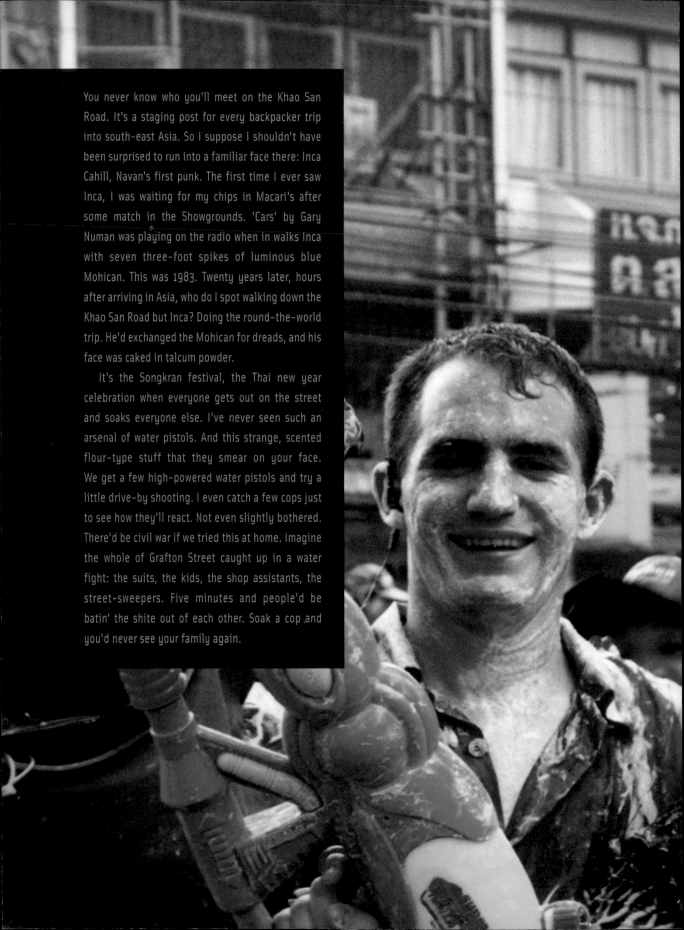

You never know who you'll meet on the Khao San Road. It's a staging post for every backpacker trip into south-east Asia. So I suppose I shouldn't have been surprised to run into a familiar face there: Inca Cahill, Navan's first punk. The first time I ever saw Inca, I was waiting for my chips in Macari's after some match in the Showgrounds. 'Cars' by Gary Numan was playing on the radio when in walks Inca with seven three-foot spikes of luminous blue Mohican. This was 1983. Twenty years later, hours after arriving in Asia, who do I spot walking down the Khao San Road but Inca? Doing the round-the-world trip. He'd exchanged the Mohican for dreads, and his face was caked in talcum powder.

It's the Songkran festival, the Thai new year celebration when everyone gets out on the street and soaks everyone else. I've never seen such an arsenal of water pistols. And this strange, scented flour-type stuff that they smear on your face. We get a few high-powered water pistols and try a little drive-by shooting. I even catch a few cops just to see how they'll react. Not even slightly bothered. There'd be civil war if we tried this at home. Imagine the whole of Grafton Street caught up in a water fight: the suits, the kids, the shop assistants, the street-sweepers. Five minutes and people'd be batin' the shite out of each other. Soak a cop .and you'd never see your family again.

The Mambo Club *is something else you'll never find at home. It's the ladyboy cabaret, where the buachaill cailíní get the chance to strut their highly confusing stuff. In hot pants and micro-minis, feathers, spandex, silk and fur, they're sashaying back and forth across the stage, miming to Abba, the Village People, Madonna and Destiny's Child. You'd think a troupe of miming transvestites wouldn't be to everyone's taste, but they're going wild for it here.* When the boys start into 'It's Raining Men', everyone goes stone mad. And it's not just the tourists either. The Thais are suckers for glitz. The theatre – a big, old-fashioned dome in heavy red velvet and gold leaf – is packed to the gills with grinning locals, clapping hands and singing along.

Backstage is a strange, strange world. Half-dressed ladyboys are zipping around, carrying costumes and props, jabbering at each other in Thai. There's just no room for the rails upon rails of gear; dresses, suits, feather boas, weird-looking underwear, all kinds of unidentifiable frills. There's that sickly smell of cheap perfume and Johnson's baby powder. Wedged into this claustrophobic little world, each performer has their own tiny dressing table with the mirrors and the light bulbs. They're hunched over them, passing around jars and bottles of slap, painting on the eyebrows and gluing on the fake nails and lashes. Confusion reigns. As well as boys dressed up as girls, this show has girls dressed up as boys. With everyone wandering around half clad, you don't know what the hell you're looking at. A girl halfway to being a boy or a boy halfway to being a girl. Buachaill cailín? Cailín buachaill? And yeah, many of these lads have moved the thing up to a whole new level and have had the lad surgically removed. Which ones? Checking out the crotch area gives no clue. If the lad remains, he's taped up and strapped back so that all you've got is this smooth expanse of gusset. Probably not a good idea to do too much staring. And it's not all wispy little effeminate lads either. You've ladyboys to suit all tastes. There are great hairy bastards with

big shoulders like legs of mutton and they're there lathering on the make-up the same as everyone else. There's this one blimp, this Jabba the Hut ladyboy holding court in one corner. Every time the camera catches him, he winks and gives it the tongue. Shudder. He had some kind of senior position in the ensemble, so they insisted I meet him. He wanted me to sit on his lap. I sat on his lap all right, so I did.

There's the obligatory camp floor manager, bouncing around, ushering people on stage. 'Come on, Hector! Come on, come on, come on, COME ON! . . . ' This was the thing. They expected me to tog off and go on.

What to wear? They dragged this yoke out of mothballs. A half-man/half-woman thing. One side screaming pink ball gown, the other a sedate black tux. It looked like something that had spent fifty years in some chest in the back of a parochial hall in Tullamore. Damp, smelly as the bejaysus. *I was about to unzip the jeans when I remembered I was travelling commando. Boxers and tropical heat don't mix, so I had flung the last pair into the far corner of the suitcase back at the hotel. Jimmy, the lad charged with looking after my make-up, solved the problem with a fetching pair of* **leather hot pants***. I tried not think about where they might have been before.*

He gets to work on the make-up, which is this mucky-looking Thai paste. I'm thinking rash city. I'll probably have to go at it with a belt sander in the morning. In jig-time I'm got up like something out of a horror film. The sorry offspring of a threesome between Bosco, Lily Savage and an emperor penguin. The floor manager hooks me up with this young fella in sequins, and we sweep out on to the stage. No one runs screaming from the place. Must be losing my touch.

If you ever need to pick up a packet of johnnies in Thailand, what you need to ask for is a pack of Mechais (pronounced mee-chighs). Mechai is the guy who spearheaded a huge family-planning drive in Thailand thirty years ago. Back then, they were averaging seven kids per family, and the economy couldn't cope. Mechai became the public face of the 'Stop at Two' campaign. The aim was to make condoms as common as cabbages way out in the Thai sticks. That's what he calls his chain of restaurants today: Cabbages and Condoms. He took me round his restaurant HQ in Bangkok. The family-planning theme is everywhere; posters, framed condoms, t-shirts. He even has 'a set of incisional vasectomy equipment' on display. It's enough to put you off your cabbage.

'We have vasectomy picnics and fairs,' says Mechai. 'The kids bring their fathers, about 200 every year, on the 5th of December, Father's Day. You've a playground for the kids and a vasectomy for the father. They have a great time.' Youch. I presented him with an Irish rubber johnny. A couple of years later, I got a text from a friend who was passing through Bangkok and dropped into the restaurant. There was my johnny, framed on the wall.

Think it would work here? Outside Kinnegad, big truckstop: 'Rashers and Rubbers'.

> 'THE SOUND GUY IS THERE HOLDING THE BOOM OVER THE ACTION AND YAWNING. HE'S GOT THIS LOOK ON HIS FACE LIKE HE'S WONDERING IF HE'LL HAVE BROCCOLI OR CARROTS WITH HIS DINNER. I, ON THE OTHER HAND, AM NOT BORED. **I AM STRUGGLING TO MAINTAIN MY PROFESSIONAL COMPOSURE WHILE THERE IN FRONT OF ME, THIS LAD IS RIDING THE HOLE OFF THIS GORGEOUS YOUNG ONE.**'

SAN FERNANDO VALLEY

'YOU KNOW WHAT I NEED?' says Chichi. 'I need a little more softcore from the standing doggie to the piledriver… Yes… Drop her the other way, Chris, atta boy… Beautiful!…Turn your face this way baby. Yes!…Right in between 'em, Chris, put your face right in between 'em. Titties all over the face. Yes! That's beautiful, kids!'

Chichi Larue, twenty stone of Los Angeles drag queen, is sitting back in his director's chair bawling instructions in a bored kind of voice. He's not in character today, so he looks like an ordinary guy. Everyone on the set looks ordinary. Everybody, in fact, looks kind of bored. The sound guy is there holding the boom over the action and yawning. He's got this look on his face like he's wondering if he'll have broccoli or carrots with his dinner. I, on the other hand, am not bored. I am struggling to maintain my professional composure while there in front of me, this lad is riding the hole off this gorgeous young one.

We're in an ordinary warehouse in an ordinary industrial estate in the San Fernando Valley, most of which is pretty ordinary too. An ordinary warehouse just like you'd see outside Kells or Kilkenny or Birr. Except, instead of computer parts or refrigerated meat, you've riding. Loads and loads of riding. Over on the other side of the hill in Hollywood, they turn out one film every couple of weeks. Here in porno valley, it's twenty a week. Ordinary people churning out ordinary films full of riding.

San Fernando itself is a Milton Keynes, a nothing-ever-happens sort of town. Take a walk down the main street and you won't notice anything unusual. Glance up at the second-floor windows, however, and you'll get an inkling of what keeps the place going. Casting agents, modelling agents – every second building. Jim South is one of the most experienced in the industry. About fifty-five, slicked-back hair, thick *Magnum*

PI moustache. I'm not there two minutes before he excuses himself to answer the phone. 'What the hell did you say to Lorne Phoenix? Does she wanna do anal?' Once he sorts out Lorne's difficulties, Jim has a lot to say in defence of the adult film business. That what it's called, by the way. It's adult film, not porn. 'Let me tell you something about this business. What the public don't realize, you have people who are very good in this business, and like any other business you have people who are not good. You have everything from conservative Republicans to liberal Democrats. You have people who believe in God in this business. The old thing that John Q Public believes that we have sex with our children and beat our wives is garbage. It's just like any other place, except it's the adult film business.'

There's a constant stream of girls in and out of the office; dropping off CVs, picking up assignments. At one point, Jim has to go next door 'for a viewing'. I get talking to a few of the actresses on their way through. 'When I first started out,' one of them tells me, 'I would only work with certain guys, only guys I was really attracted to. Now I just programme myself. It's all work. I have to enjoy myself even if I don't.'

'For a viewing', 'working' – in San Fernando, almost anything can mean riding.

Back on set, the crew is setting up for this Roman garden scene. Chichi is standing in the middle of a group of stage hands, trying different arrangements of plants and pillars. There's another guy at the top of a ladder, adjusting lights. Trevor, this real clean-cut college-guy type, is getting ready for his scene with Sunrise Adams. He's a male porn star and, get this, he's married. 'You know, Hector,' he says, 'the hardest thing for me is to leave some in the tank for my missus. I've just had sex with a beautiful woman for five hours. I've got to switch off and go home.' Can you imagine this in Ireland? Back from a hard day at the orifice, and the wife asks how was the traffic and did you ride anyone nice today?

But trouble strikes before things get too far along. The cry goes up from the set: 'Wood is gone! Wood is down!' Níl lad an lad ag obair. Shaking his head and tying on his dressing gown, Trevor is ushered out a side door.

The uncooperative lad is of course the bane of the porn industry. Earlier, in Jim South's office, one of the longest-serving male porn stars in the business, Steve Austin – the Six Million Dollar Man – recalled his first 'acting' job. 'After a few counselling sessions I was able to forget about it, but Buck, the director, said to me, Steve, whenever you want to get wood it would be really nice because we're losing fucking daylight. That doesn't help an actor who's struggling.'

Then there's the opposite problem. 'I've probably done about forty scenes,' says Trevor, 'and there are probably two where I've popped early. What we did is we took a break for about thirty minutes, then cranked up the engine again. If you let the cameraman know you're about to pop, even if it's early, then they can get it on film, then they can edit it so you don't have to do it a second time.'

FOR THE RECORD, BOYS, TREVOR SAYS **SIZE ISN'T THE THING: 'I DON'T THINK SO. IT'S ABOUT PERFORMANCE.** AS FAR AS THE SCENES ARE CONCERNED, IT'S ABOUT PERFORMANCE.'

For the record, boys, Trevor says size isn't the thing: 'I don't think so. It's about performance. As far as the scenes are concerned, it's about performance.' As soon as he regains his composure, performance is what we get. Chichi leans back in his chair and says to me. 'You enjoying this, Hector?' I'm remembering the first dodgy film I ever saw. *Emmanuelle*. They made a whole string of these things in the seventies and eighties. Of course it's harmless by today's standards – you'll see racier stuff on Ros na Rún and it's nothing compared to what Sunrise and Trevor are getting up to over on the top of that balustrade. Anyway, back when I was working in Coláiste na bhFiann, there was this one summer where myself and my mate Risteard had to come in a couple of days early to get the school ready before everyone else arrived. A couple of days with the whole, vast boarding school all to ourselves. So we went downtown, bought about ten bottles of Ritz and rented ourselves a scannán gorm. Exploring the place earlier, we'd found a video player in one of the priest's rooms – they were all off on holidays – so we watched it in there, but at two o'clock in the morning in a deserted boarding school, it became the scariest film we ever saw. Every couple of minutes it was, ssshhhh, did you hear that? I think someone's coming!

'Lemme hear you, guys!' Chichi barks.

Stretched out on the balustrade, Sunrise gets louder. Trevor redoubles his efforts. On cue, he executes what's known in the business as a 'fake internal pop'..

'That's beautiful kids, beautiful! Take a break!'

There's not much plot to these things. Boy meets girl. Boy goes down on girl. Girl goes down on boy. They ride. 'That's basically the A to Z kind of thing,' Chichi admits when I corner him during the break. 'But I add my Chichi personality to the scene. I'm the cheerleader. I'm the screamer, I'm the one who gets the spit!'

The film itself is a Vivid production – we're here as guests of Vivid – and as far as hardcore pornography goes, their stuff is relatively mild. Nice even. *Good production values, good cinematography. Their scenes are nearly always boy-girl, very rarely girl-girl and never boy-boy-boy-boy-boy-boy-girl. 'There's regular films and there's gonzo films,' Mercedez explains. She's just arrived on set and we're about to watch her have sex on top of a white convertible. Gonzo? 'That's when you have twelve guys doing an anal gangbang,' she says, kind of embarrassed. 'That's not Vivid. This is condom only, it's very safe, it's very classy.'*

As herself and Chris – Chris Cannon – get stuck in, so does our cameraman, Enda. We'd been instructed by Vivid to remove the zoom lens, to keep back from the action and just take wide-angle shots. Close-ups were forbidden. Enda, though, ah . . . he forgot. That night, the camera gets passed round between the hotel rooms as, professionals that we are, we review the day's material. Thoroughly.

'Hola, Señor Hector! Housekeeping!'

'No gracias! I'm OK! Just leave the towels outside the door...'

LAS VEGAS

'SEE THAT?' says Rock, holding up a scrap of paper. 'That's what it's all about.' Rock Miller. Real name? God knows. Probably Cedric Crapplebottom or something. It's a note he's got in his hand: from Andrea. Her phone number. 'I'm a busy girl, call me tonight if you're not!' Are you going to use it? I ask him. He raises one perfectly formed eyebrow, curls one perfectly formed lip and shrugs. 'I might,' says he, folding it up and putting it back in the arse pocket of his jeans.

Such is the life of a Chippendale.

I've been in dressing rooms before but never one like this. Where are the Dunne's Stores bags full of gear? Where's the lad hopping his boot off the ground trying to get the grass out? There's nobody going around trying to get the names in Irish for the referee, nobody saying, 'This is just the team we're startin with, lads. If it's not workin out there's plenty of changes we can make.' Rock's giving himself a smouldering look in the mirror, running the hair-dryer over his quiff. It's all leather trousers, glistening pecs, these cutaway cuffs and collars – no shirt – and a little bow-tie like a cherry on a cake. Instead of deep heat, the place smells like a French cathouse. There's g-strings instead of jock-straps. Nobody's ugly. These boys, let's be honest, are beautiful. I mean, I'm as straight as the next man, but by Jesus, if you're not 100 per cent committed to the heterosexual lifestyle, these boys will turn you.

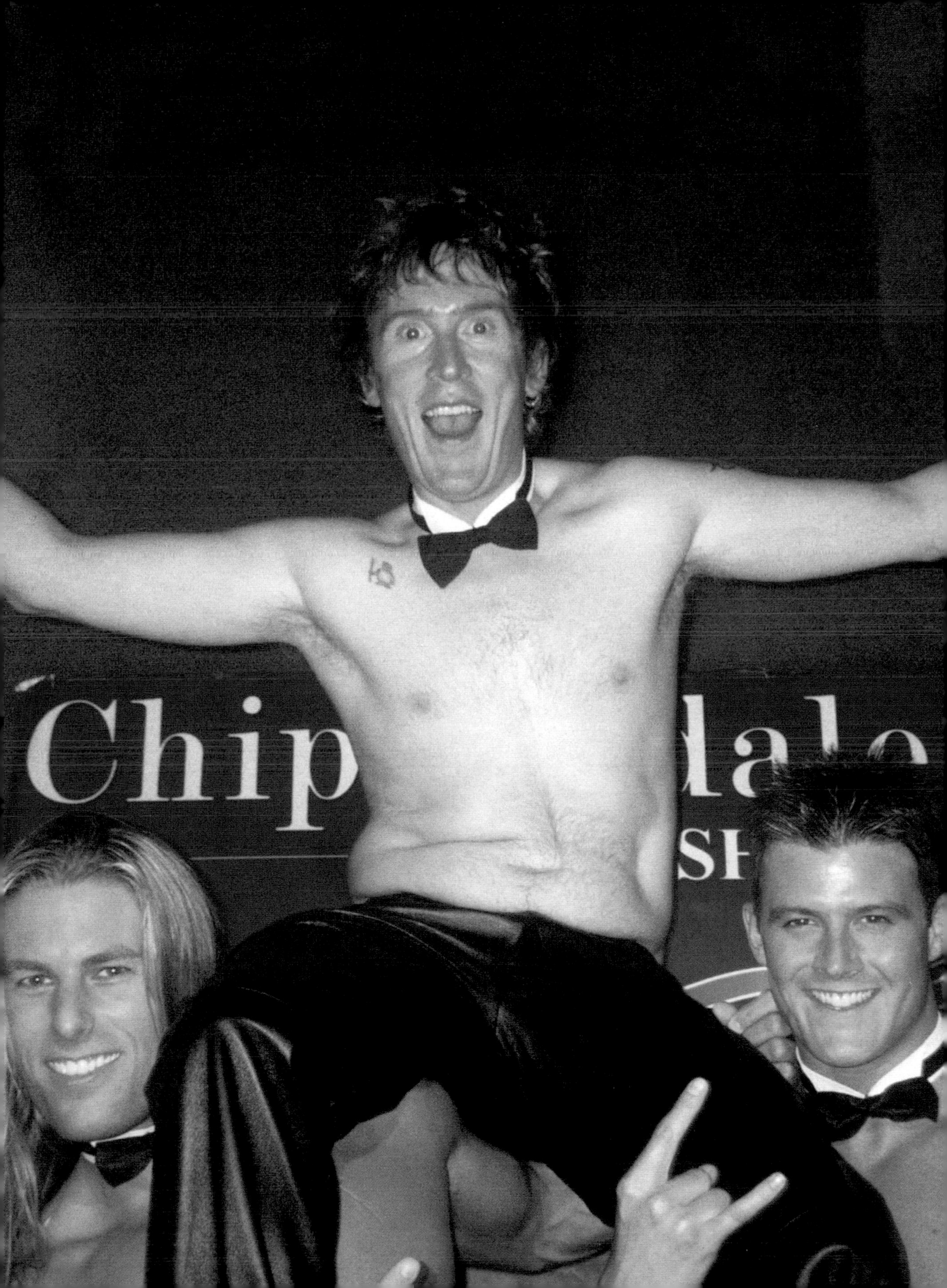

'FIRST NIGHT, I SIT IN ON A SHOW
AND IT HITS ME STRAIGHT AWAY.
**THIS ISN'T JUST STRUT, STRUT,
THRUST, RIP OFF TROUSERS.**
THESE GUYS CAN DANCE, THESE
GUYS CAN PERFORM.'

We're installed in the Hotel Rio in Las Vegas. Over 2,500 rooms, dozens of restaurants, a casino bigger than Croke Park and a mock Italian village for shopping in. Down in the lobby, it's like Tramore or Salthill. Oul wans with flowerpots full of two pences working the slots. For entertainment, you've everything from a year-round beach party in Bikini's Beach and Dance Club to the best male strippers in the world. *The Chippendales have agreed, not alone to let me hang around with them for the week, but also to get up on stage and perform with them on Saturday night. In front of 700 screaming women. The only worry is that they'll be screaming for all the wrong reasons when they behold Hector in a g-string.*

Kevin, one of the elder statesmen of the group, meets me at the airport. Even though he's holding a sign with my name on it, there's no mistaking the Chippendale at the arrivals gate. Six-three or four, chest bursting out of his sweatshirt, long blond hair and face carved out of granite. In the limo in from the airport, he puts Queens of the Stone Age on the stereo. Class.

'I ran into some rock stars,' he tells me, 'on a plane back from Europe. I was like, oh my God, it's Whitesnake! I told them I would love to be a rock star. They said yeah? What do you do? I said I work for the Chippendales. Guy says, fuck you, man, you've got 100 per cent female audience, we've got 75 per cent male. I wanna be you!' Himself and Nathan, another long-serving member, take myself and the crew out for a meal on their night off. The adulation they get is something else. Up in Caesar's Palace's famous Shadow Bar, there's women throwing themselves at them. I ask Nathan if he can have sex with a woman every night of the week. 'You can. Most definitely. You can. The option is yours. A, B or C. If you want the A, you may have to work that little bit harder, but Cs are easy to go home with.'

'For five years I've been with the Chippendales,' says Kevin, 'and I had a serious relationship for one. That was the first year I was working here. After that, it's gone to hell. You're constantly surrounded by women. There's always temptation.'

First night, I sit in on a show and it hits me straight away. This isn't just strut, strut,

‟TO GET UP ON STAGE AND PERFORM
WITH THEM ON SATURDAY NIGHT.
IN FRONT OF **700 SCREAMING WOMEN**.
THE ONLY WORRY IS THAT THEY'LL BE
SCREAMING FOR ALL THE WRONG
REASONS WHEN THEY BEHOLD
HECTOR IN A G-STRING.„

thrust, rip off trousers. These guys can dance, these guys can perform. The show starts a good hour before they actually come on. They've big screens up all round the hall, running slide shows of the boys in various stages of undress. One man per screen, you can read about his hobbies, his favourite food, his star sign. With about fifteen minutes to go, the music pumping and the drink flowing, they send in the mini-Chippendales. Oompa Loompas, but well-built Oompa Loompas, there to start the juices flowing before the main course. They're showing the busloads of women to their seats, they're giving massages and backrubs.

Then the countdown, and the boys hit the boards. All fantasies are catered for: you've the cowboy, the Wall Street exec, the Harvard boy, the Hispanic, the army officer . . . Just wait 'til Saturday night, when they get a load of the FCA officer.

Trouble is, your average Irishman isn't at home on the dancefloor. Everything I know about dance I learned in Diamonds Niteclub in Navan in the late eighties. Doing the Jim Kerr impressions to 'Don't You Forget About Me'. Trying to score a shift to Simply Red's 'Holding Back The Years'. You don't really dance in slow-sets of course. It's more of a shuffle round the floor, trying to manoeuvre the gob into the right place. There's going to have to be a lot of improvement in the next five days to keep the salivating women in the theatre of the Hotel Rio from looking for their fifty (fifty!) bucks back.

One of the highlights – that has the women half out of their minds – is Kevin writhing naked on this big iron bedstead. Or at least he gives the impression of being naked. This is an essential part of the show. No cocks. Or at least no cocks on display. Your cocksock is standard issue. You titillate and tease, you cup and thrust, but the lad is kept under wraps at all times. That way they can say it's tasteful. So there's Kevin, grinding away on these white silk sheets, straddling and pumping, tossing the long blond hair behind him like it's an ad for Timotei. When the jocks come flying off, it seems like the screaming is going to structurally damage the place. The young one beside me looks like she might explode. There's underwear and scraps of paper with phone numbers on landing on the stage like confetti at a wedding.

Preparation for my stripping debut (OK, not exactly debut, but it's the first time to a paying audience) begins when I meet Nathan and Kevin at the gym next morning. I've my original Hank Traynor jersey, the jersey he wore in the famous 2003 replay victory over Westmeath, to inspire feats of superhuman power and endurance. 'Who the fuck is Hank Traynor?' says Kevin. Words I never thought I'd hear. It's like getting a quarterback jersey from the Dallas Cowboys, I tell him, or Halle Berry's bikini when she came out of the water that time, or LeBron James' jocks or Tiger Wood's sweat bands. They seem to get the idea.

As soon as we get stuck into the workout, it becomes pretty obvious that I'm not really in the same league. While the boys are throwing seventy-pound dumb-bells around for fun, I'm sweating under two twenty-pounders. But OK, there was never any chance I was going to bulk up in three days. A little personal grooming, however, can work wonders. Waxing? No thanks. I just trim a few of the more brillo-like nipple hairs and I'm a new man. And tanning? Fuck that. About time the ladies of Las Vegas saw what colour a real man looks like. Blue-veined, see-through skin, plenty of ginger forestation in the right places and, of course, the freckles. Millions of them. Join the dots and find the Irishman.

To beef up the numbers and give the show a bit of cabaret polish, the eleven Chippendales are joined on stage by about eighteen professional dancers for the bigger numbers. Wes is the main man here. He dances with Celine Dion on a Monday night, the Chippendales on Tuesday and gives dance classes the rest of the time. Wes, God love him, has been given the job of turning me into a reasonable mover within two days. He takes me through the choreography, which is bloody complicated and bloody fast. Any chance they might consider replacing the upbeat poprock number we're supposed to be doing with 'Holding Back the Years'? I demonstrate the shuffle shuffle slurp technique perfected in Diamonds. Wes doesn't think they'll go for it.

Can't help but get a little nervous now. This routine calls for a lot of groin cupping, body stroking, pelvic gyration and hip-thrusting. As any Irishwoman will tell you, Irishmen can't pull this kind of shit off. More than that, though, you can be out of sync and get away with it, or you can be wildly out of sync and fuck the whole thing up for everybody. I'm sure the producers are on to Wes the whole time, trying to find out if this Irish guy is going to make a pig's arse of the entire show.

Bobby is the Chippendale's wardrobe man. 'The object of this,' he says, holding up a black g-string, 'is to keep the king of the leprechauns at bay.' A Chippendale is not a Chippendale without his g-string, and I'm here to be fitted for mine. When I tell him that it's boxers I'm more used to, he tells me to think of it as a boxer gone on vacation. The g-string, more comfortable than you'd imagine, does the necessary job, but there's a still significant ginger foliage that the skimpy black cotton can't contain. 'Well, it's red,' says Nathan, who likes to keep his own jungle from encroaching with a razor, 'so you can't really see it.' Bobby gives me the trademark collar and cuffs, the dickie bow. I look like a snooker player fallen on hard times. 'You look great dog,' Nathan reassures. 'You'll do fine.'

All Saturday afternoon, I'm in the hotel room going over the routine. I had to learn the thing in slow motion, and speeding it up isn't all that easy. Punch punch, grope, flail, thrust, sashay, punch. After a few pointers from Kevin and one of the other dancers, Jeff, the final rehearsal goes well. In the dressing room before going on, everyone's stoked up. The sight of Hector in his g-string turns them all into comedians. 'You've got it on sideways, fucker!' says Kevin. Sure, they're all jealous.

Waiting in the wings while the boys do the first number, I miss my cue. I'm halfway on to the bloody stage before I realize I'm not supposed to be there. Quick about turn, and strut off, making out as if it was all part of the act. Then, bang, we're on. And it's over. In seconds. Goes perfectly. No one thrown off course, no one loses an eye. In the final move, I swagger up to the front of the stage and beckon all the boys to gather round. Everyone freezes in perfect sync as the music ends. OK. Can't resist my own little improvisation. I turn around and unbuckle the pants. The pale moon rises once again. **'There ye are, girls, here's a slice of Royal Power!' Vegas explodes into spontaneous applause.**

PLAYBOY MANSION

HEFNER WAS LATE. This wouldn't have been a problem under normal circumstances, but then these weren't normal circumstances. Four months, it took us to get here. Emails, phone calls, carrier pigeons back and forth between Galway and his publicist in Chicago. In the end, they said we could have five hours. Five hours in the Playboy Mansion may sound like a fine thing, but this was five hours of shooting for a twenty-six minute show. Usually, we get five days. We had only one shot. Get in, get rolling, squeeze as much interest/crack/lunacy out of it as possible.

The publicist – Rob – met us at the door. 'Mr Hefner has been delayed,' he told us. Dressed in chinos and a novelty tie, Rob was your typical publicist. Slightly camp, 100-watt smile, bursting with energy. 'He should be down in half an hour.' We were shown into the library. Huge, gothic affair, like something out of *The Munsters*, all thick, heavy velvet and floor-to-ceiling books. While Enda set the cameras up, I watched the time run down. Tick, tick, tick… Rob got busy choreographing the set-up. 'You will sit here behind the camera, Mr Hefner will take his place here on the chaise, the cameras will be positioned here…' That's not how I usually do it, I tell him. It's not *Today Tonight*. Can I not just sit down there beside him, have the chat, like? He blinked, a this-is-highly-unorthodox blink, then seemed to change his mind. 'Sure, OK.'

Check the time. Twenty minutes to Hefner's arrival. About now the feeling started to build. I tried to ignore it, like you do, but it wouldn't go away. Fifteen minutes. Starting to hurt now. At five minutes, there was no arguing any more. Hugh Hefner or no Hugh Hefner, TV show or no TV show, I had to…ah…go.

Now. One of my first TV gigs was a kids' show on TV3. I learned the golden rule there. Turn off your mike when you're not on camera. Leave on your mike and everyone

in the studio will hear every tiny detail of everything you do no matter where you are on set. Forgot the golden rule in the jacks in the Playboy Mansion. Enda, who had the headphones on, realizes what has happened straight away, but instead of rushing out to tip me off, he sets up facing the door of said jacks, so as to capture the full embarrassment as I come out. Hugh Hefner meanwhile, the playboy of the western world, clad in trademark gun-metal pyjamas, sweeps down to the library to find me gone. 'I'm sorry, Mr Hefner,' says Rónan, the producer, 'our presenter's in the jacks.' Says Hefner, smooth as you like, 'The call of nature comes to us all.' Meanwhile, sitting astride the coolest black marble that dollars can buy, I'm making free with Mr Hefner's toiletries. It's all black marble: the can, the walls, the ceiling… There are gold taps, umpteen different sprays and aftershaves: Boss, Gucci, you name it. All embossed with the Playmate logo. Best of all, though, best of all…a golden canister of cotton buds.

I have a cotton bud fixation. When we did the show up in Helsinki, we were in this place, the Harrods of Finland, called Stockmans. They say you can buy anything there, from a needle to an anchor, a Ferrari to a tube of tomato purée. Your one said to me, Hector, you tell me three things and I will tell you if we have them or not, so I said right, give me a CD of Daniel O'Donnell, give me boxer shorts of the Simpsons and show me your range of cotton buds. They had the Simpsons, they hadn't Daniel O'Donnell but they had

> **MEANWHILE, SITTING ASTRIDE THE COOLEST BLACK MARBLE THAT DOLLARS CAN BUY, I'M MAKING FREE WITH MR HEFNER'S TOILETRIES. BEST OF ALL, THOUGH, BEST OF ALL... A GOLDEN CANISTER OF COTTON BUDS.**
>
> ## I HAVE A COTTON BUD FIXATION.

about forty different types of cotton buds. So now I'm sitting inside there, the interview forgotten, busily excavating the ears with Hefner's premium-grade cotton buds.

Sorry about that, Mr Hefner, sorry about that. 'No problem,' he goes. He didn't know what to make of me. So, I asked him, is there ever any hassle in the castle? 'Heh heh,' he says, 'I like this guy.' Panic over. Situation saved. We'd sent him the Taiwan show – the one with the weights agus na liathróidí – via his publicist, just so's he could get an idea of the kind of programme it was. They told us he loved it, this red-headed guy speaking Gaelic with the dangling weights and the rest of it. He said, sure, we'll do it, get the guy over here...

So now. The question everyone asks. In Tesco's, in the pub, in the jacks, on the street... lads at the races especially. Hector, what was the Playboy Mansion like? There's this glint in the eye. No mistaking what they're really asking. You have this idea that inside those doors, all kinds of wild, rampant sexual antics are going on night and day. Well, neither sight nor sound of it did I see. Closest I got was rubbing up against a flamingo in the garden when Holly – his favourite girl – was showing me around the grounds. Hef told me he wasn't happy married to his first wife. 'I felt as if my life was over to some extent. I felt as if I was going to turn into my parents.' He had this fantasy of living in a big house with loads of girls. That's what they want you to believe, that he's made that fantasy real. This is the HQ of the Playboy brand. It's all about the image. Getting it out there. When he shows up at some Saturday-night première with seven platinum blondes on his arm, a pound to a penny there'll be pictures in the papers on the Monday.

I asked him, did you have sex last night? He says, I did. I asked him how do you choose the girl, is it Monday, Tuesday and so on? He said, no, I have sex with maybe three different girls a week. Holly I have sex with more at the moment because she's my favourite.

I said, tell me about last night, did you take Viagra? He says, I did, I took it about eight o'clock in the evening, we watched a movie, had a glass of wine, had sex.

He was completely candid about it. Is it true? Who knows? The parties, we were told, were cracked altogether. They'd gather up the hopeful young things, the young ones around town looking for a break, bring them up to the mansion, let them hang around with the rock stars, the film stars, let nature take its course... Is it true? Who knows.

Hef himself is a legend. IQ of 152 – that's genius. He produced the first issue of Playboy in 1953 on $8,000 borrowed from friends and family. In 1971, it sold seven million copies. Seven million. It was the best-selling magazine in the world. His daughter looks after the empire these days, but he's still got his finger on the pulse. The whole time we were there, he had cameras on us. He's got this old guy, Roger, on retainer, to tail everybody who comes into the place. When Nelly and Justin Timberlake were in doing that video, Roger was somewhere in the background with the camera rolling. He's a film nut, Hefner. He's got something like 40,000 tapes in his private archive, plus footage of everything that's ever happened at the mansion. We talked about the Irish market and how the magazine's been doing since the ban was lifted in 1995. Of course nowadays, there's all kinds of stuff on the top shelf, and *Playboy* is tame by comparison, but not when I was a chap. We had one porn magazine in my class in first year in St Pat's, passed around between everyone. I was so terrified of my mam finding it, I hid it in the woods about two miles from the house, buried in a plastic bag to keep it dry. Years later, I took a walk down memory lane, went back down to the woods, and there were the remnants of it. You could just about make out arms and legs.

So, while the daughter is running the business, the man himself is taking care of the brand – he got Holly to dress up in the suit and show us around. Holly Madison, from Craig, Alaska. His favourite girl. The week before we were there, she had her father, mother and her granny, all staying in the Playboy mansion. What did they make of it? 'They thought it was great, they loved it. My mom loved LA.' Could you imagine this at home? I'm off to Killiney to dress in a bunny suit and live with a geriatric millionaire and his half-dozen other girlfriends? Could you imagine your ma and your da and your granny coming up from Cloughjordan for the weekend and thinking it was all ceart go leor?

She took me round, gave me the full Cribs tour. Hefner had two kids with his second wife, Kimberly. After they separated, he set herself and the kids up in a house just over the wall from the mansion. They're in and out the whole time. I met the son in the games room, about twelve years old, playing space invaders. What must it be like to be him? I mean, there's this huge bronze bust of his ma in the hallway. With everything on display, like. Can you imagine what he's going to be like at fifteen or sixteen? Drinking a couple of Royal Dutch outside with

BUT THE PARTIES. THE THING WAS, THE THING WE ALL KNEW, WAS THAT SATURDAY, HE WAS GOING TO BE SEVENTY-SEVEN YEARS OLD. BIG, BIG PARTY IN THE PLAYBOY MANSION. EVERYONE WAS GOING TO BE THERE. JUSTIN TIMBERLAKE, LIMP BISKIT, COLIN FARRELL. HECTOR WAS ANGLING FOR THE INVITE.

his mates, saying, lads, ye have to check this out, the oul fella's got a party going on, wait till you see what they're at!

The games room was something else. Pinball, Pac-man, Asteroids, Foosball. There was a room off it that I'd seen in Cribs. Holly goes, 'Hector, this is where everyone comes and relaxes, it's very private, they can play games and then, if they want, they can get one-on-one.' She wasn't talking about basketball. The room was one big couch. You take off your shoes and it's all bouncy and mattressy, all leather and soft lighting. Outside, the place is a zoo, literally. He's got a zoo permit and keeps pheasants, flamingos, parrots, monkeys, and real bunnies too. The pool had this amazing 'grotto', Holly called it, like the most luxurious spa you've ever been in. You could only access it through this underwater tunnel from the pool. It had little rockpools, there were candles everywhere and ornate shelves for your towels, slippers, robes and the rest of it. You can imagine the shenanigans that go on here during these parties. Jaysus, I said to Holly, you could do some damage in here. She spins round, 'My God, Hector, what's wrong, is something broken, is everything OK?' She came across as innocent and shrewd at the same time. For her this was it, this was making it . . . I asked her if she'd marry him, she got really serious, said, sure, she'd love to, she'd marry him in the morning. There were rumours afterwards that they were going to get married, but nothing came of it. He's downsized to just three girls now, but Holly's still hanging on, still got that coveted favourite-girl tag.

But the parties. The thing was, the thing we all knew, was that Saturday, he was going to be seventy-seven years old. Big, big party in the Playboy Mansion. Everyone was going to be there. Justin Timberlake, Limp Biskit, Colin Farrell. Hector was angling for the invite. Half an hour in, with the interview going great, I upped the stakes. I produced a bottle of vintage Irish whiskey. On behalf of all Irish lads, thanks for all the pleasure you've given us down the years. I thought, in that moment he'd say something like, 'Hector, we're having a party Saturday night, you guys are all right, you gonna be around?' But do you think he did?

We were in a Chinese in downtown Hollywood on Saturday night. The only bunnies were in the food.

> 'SNAILS IN FRANCE, CROCODILE HEAD IN THE AMAZON, MINKE WHALE WITH THE *RAINBOW WARRIOR* BOYS IN ICELAND. **I GOBBLED DOWN A BIG FAT PENIS IN CHILE – IN AN EROTIC CAKE SHOP. THE TWO THAT REALLY STAND OUT THOUGH ARE THE FROG MILKSHAKE IN PERU AND THE DEEP FRIED LOCUSTS IN BEIJING.**'

WEIRD FOOD

SNAILS IN FRANCE, crocodile head in the Amazon, minke whale with the *Rainbow Warrior* boys in Iceland. I gobbled down a big fat penis in Chile – in an erotic cake shop. The two that really stand out though are the frog milkshake in Peru and the deep fried locusts in Beijing.

Lima. The most boring city in South America. Possibly the world. We were saved by two tourist cops. One thing Lima has in abundance is cops – of all makes and models. You've one force for security, another to deal with accidents and emergencies; even one to deal with explosions. The two tourist cops spotted us and came over. How's it going they said, do you need anything? We told them we were about to drop dead of boredom. Is there anything vaguely interesting happening anywhere in town? The cop thought about it for a minute, then grinned. Come with me, he says. Off we went out of the main square, over the bridge and down into a rougher part of the city, arriving eventually at this ordinary little shop on an ordinary little side street. 'Aquí,' says the cop, pointing to the queue of pasty looking chaps lined up in the shop's gloomy interior. 'Los batidos de rana.'

'Qué?' I said, not sure I'd heard him right.

'Los batidos de rana.'

Frog milkshakes. Are you serious?

It's for health, says the cop, shrugging.

The first thing to notice was the large tank full of squirming frogs on the counter. The second thing was the large glass blender beside it. In front of the counter, a queue of lads sniffling, coughing, looking beat up and run down. The guy behind the counter, by contrast, is full of beans. Bustling about chatting with the boys. As we walk in,

he reaches into the frog tank and fishes one out. Holding it between index finger and thumb, he presents it to the customer at the head of the queue. The frog, doing his living best to wriggle out of your man's hand, looks up at the customer with his little froggy eyes. The customer looks down at the frog. 'Yup,' he says. 'He'll do.'

Your man reaches under the counter, takes out a short knife and whaps the frog twice on the on the back of the head with the flat of it. He then runs the edge of the blade down along the frog's back, leaving a neat little incision bordered by two flaps of loose froggy skin. He drops the knife, grabs one of these flaps and pulls. The skin comes away in one fluid motion. The frog is basically turned inside out. Next he flips it round, another flick of the knife and out come the frog's innards. The gutted, skinned frog is dropped into the blender.

There he lies, glistening, big blue eyes shining up at us. Though I find this hard to believe, the shopkeeper tells us that he's still alive. I stare at him a minute and see one of his legs twitch. To the half-dead frog he now adds a whole heap of herbs, eggs, roots and boiling stock, along with something that smells like whiskey. He covers the top of the blender with one hand and with the other, he starts the thing going. 'Bit of a cough, is it José?' Buzzzzzzzzzzzzzzzz.

'Bit of a headcold, yeah?' Buzzzzzzzzzzzzzzzzzz. 'Since last Thursday? Aye, it's going around, so it is.' Buzzzzzzzzzzzzzzz. He turns it off and strains the mixture into a bowl, then takes a plastic cup and pours it in. José grabs it and glugs it down in one.

Rosco is having trouble keeping the camera focused on this. He's gagging silently as he watches your man shlurp the frog juice, a little stream of the grey-brown gloop snaking down his stubbly chin.

Your man says to me, what do you want? I said I'm not sick, what can you do for me? He said, you want one for this area? For fertility? Keep your cock hard? Or I can give you one for energy or body cleansing.

I said give me one for energy.

Now I go through the ritual of selecting the frog. I never realized they came in so many colours. Greeny yellow, yellowy brown, browny green ... I choose a nice fat tobacco coloured lad. Whap, slice, pull, flick. In goes the twitching amphibian, followed closely by a range of other ingredients your man selects from the plastic containers packed on the shelves behind him. Buzzzzzzzzzzzzzzzzz. Strainer, cup. The moment of truth.

If I see locals doing something, I'll do it. I'll never go into an empty restaurant, no matter where it is. But if there's a crowd, whatever's coming out of the kitchen is probably all right. We're all made of the same stuff. Its not as if Peruvians have some special part of the gut dedicated to the digestion of frogs. Feck it. I took a sip ... hmmmm ... cinnamony. But if I'm going to drink it, the boys are going to drink it too. Rosco had a sip – and kept it down – as did Evan. Our two new friends, the tourist cops, they took a taste as well. Then glug glug glug, I finished it off. But apart from a vaguely amphibious, rainforest type burp, I felt the exact same afterwards as I did before I walked in.

A whole skewer of beetles, curled up around this thin wooden stake threaded through their fat, segmented bodies. Silkworms, says the guy at the stall, grinning at the look of disgust on my face. I pointed to another skewer. What are they? Frogs legs, all packed tight together on the stick. What about those little hoors? Locusts, says your man. Jesus Christ. Frogs are one thing. I don't mind them so much, I can deal with squishy, but beetles? Shudder. Remember those big black lads that'd scuttle out when you'd lift a stone. If you walked on one you could hear the crrrrraaaaack! Yuk. Still grinning broadly, your man takes the stick of locusts and drops it into the wok. The oil fizzles. A minute later, out they come, glistening and oily. He hands it over. *Íosa Chríost*, why don't I get a normal job? I close my eyes and raise it slowly to the gob. Crrrraaaack. Something oozes out. Up in the taste part of the brain, the numbskull in charge jumps to his feet. 'That's fucking beetle! Get that shit out of here now!' Over to the bin, heave up into it.

There's this little kid who's been following us as we made our way through the food stalls. He's shaking his head in disgust as I spit the last remnants of locust into the bin. And when I fire the rest of the skewer in too, he dives after it. He starts ranting at me in Chinese as he picks the flecks of rubbish off my discarded lunch. 'That's good bloody locust you fool! What you think you're doing throwing away good locust. Stupid ignorant round-eyed red-headed Caucasian freak!'

CELTS

THE IRISH ABROAD: COPS, SOLDIERS, SINGERS & DIGGERS

'YOU'D IMAGINE BEAUTIFUL WHITE BEACHES AND CLEAR BLUE SEA, BUT FRENCH GUIANA IS THIS LITTLE SCRAP OF LAND UP ON BRAZIL'S SHOULDER, RIGHT AT THE MOUTH OF THE AMAZON. EACH DAY YOU'VE MILLIONS OF TONS OF SEDIMENT WASHED DOWN THE RIVER AND DEPOSITED IN THE ATLANTIC. AND FOR HUNDREDS OF MILES EITHER SIDE OF THE MOUTH OF THE RIVER, THE SEA IS DIRTY AND BROWN.'

FRENCH GUIANA

MRS ENFIELD WAS OUR FRENCH TEACHER. We used to do this thing, if she was walking up the middle aisle, you'd reach out and see how close you could come. Derek Doyle was a master at it. A genius. He'd have his hand millimetres away, hugging the contours of her arse. He'd keep the hand there, turn round and mug back at the rest of us. One day, of course, she turned round and caught him. I never saw anything funnier. But in the first year, she threw me out of class for two weeks for messing. This might be part of the reason why I hate French so much. As soon as I could, I dropped it and did Latin instead. I hate French. I hate France. I hate Thierry Henry. I hate this va va voom. I hate the cockiness of them. I hate the pomp of them. I've been to Paris a couple of times and I hate it. I went to Père Lachaise Cemetery to see Jim Morrison's grave, I went to the Arc de Triomphe, which was good, but the rest of it you can have. Bloody French. Ooh la la mo thóin.

Who goes off to join the French Foreign Legion? Nutters, that's who. Lads who've lost the missus, lost the job, got drunk and driven the car into the canal. Or they beat the shite out of eight people outside the nightclub and went on the run. You'd hear about them every so often. The Butcher Gibney? He drank two bottles of whiskey down the Ramparts and threw his bike in through Macari's window. Before he disappeared for ever, somebody heard him shout, 'Yis can all go and fuck off, ye shower of bastards. I'm off to join the Legion.'

We were in French Guiana pretty much because of stories like that. Here, in this bizarre little colony, this thinly populated France-in-the-jungle, 2,000 miles from Europe, you've the headquarters of the Troisième Régiment Étranger d'Infanterie.

As far as I was concerned, a whole nest of loopers and misfits all packed together out in the middle of nowhere.

We drove for an hour through sweltering forty-degree heat from the capital, Cayenne, down to Kourou in the south, to where the Legion is based. The country is 90 per cent rainforest, thick and green on either side of the road. You'd imagine beautiful white beaches and clear blue sea, but French Guiana is this little scrap of land up on Brazil's shoulder, right at the mouth of the Amazon. Each day you've millions of tons of sediment washed down the river and deposited in the Atlantic. Seventy miles out from shore, it's still no more than twenty feet deep. And for hundreds of miles either side of the mouth of the river, the sea is dirty and brown, like some factory's been pumping black sludge into it. So you've stifling heat, dirty seas and absolutely fuck all to do. We were here for the Foreign Legion and the European Space Centre, but besides that the place was dead. A ghost country. Standing in the centre of Kourou in the middle of the day, I counted four people over a ten-minute period.

Dull as ditchwater. Do not go to French Guiana.

As we turned in the gates of the barracks, we saw two recruits – a guy and a girl. Dressed in fatigues, they were bent over this gleaming bronze statue of a legionnaire, cleaning it. Cleaning it with toothbrushes. They were still at it when we left late that afternoon.

Fergal was waiting for us just inside the gates. Fergal Keating from Westport. Fifteen years in the Legion. Built like a wire brush. Lean, muscled, not a spare ounce of fat. A hardy bastard. The first thing he said to me. 'I'm Fergal Keating from Westport, where men are men and the sheep are nervous.'

What is it makes a guy join the Legion, really? Is it all broken hearts and lads on the run? 'You're nineteen,' he says, 'you want to do something and you want to do something different. I sold my racing bike, bought a one-way ticket to France in 1987 and from there I just turned up, handed over my passport, in the door and bang.' It was that simple. Eighteen years on, he speaks four languages, has houses in the South of France and has seen things most people will never see. I asked him if he was the same boy who left Mayo at nineteen. 'Physically. Mentally maybe. Seen a lot of the world, seen a lot of good things in the world and seen a lot of bad things. War, conflict. Yugoslavia, Rwanda . . . The hairiest moment, we were about ten facing a hundred Rwandans. They weren't rebels, they were the local guys who were committing the massacres. We just wound up face to face on the border. They were moving back into Zaire . . . ' And what happened? He makes this half-smile, this real Irish shrug . . . 'We managed to quieten them down.'

Because we were there, they'd given Fergal a day's leave, and he was going to make the most of it. First thing, he suggested bringing us off to this training camp to see some of the new recruits being put through their paces. Into the van, out on the road. The first shop we passed, he told us to pull in. Hopped out. Two six-packs of ice-cold Heineken. Sitting in the back of the van at ten in the morning, fag in one hand, he snapped open a can and glugged it back. Then another. He took off the stiff legionnaire's peaked hat, wiped his forehead with the back of his hand and straight away he was transformed. One minute an adjutant in the French Foreign Legion, the next just another Paddy drinking his morning beer in the back of a Hiace. Adjutant, he tells us, is about the same as a sergeant major in the regular army. But what do you actually do, Fergal? Turns out he has one of the coolest job titles ever. Jungle Warfare Instructor. They all come down here to train: the SAS, the marines. I told him about the show we'd done on the marine base in North Carolina. The few, the proud – that's their motto. They believe they're best soldiers in the world.

'We've had the American marines . . . ' He makes the face you make if you're served a pint with a bad head. 'But ah . . . no helicopter, they're not happy. I'm not taking the mickey out of them, it's good to be proud, it's not good to be too proud . . . The thing about a legionnaire is, you can stick him in there, in the arsehole of the jungle, no helicopter, no air cover, nothing, and he'll come back out smiling at you.'

And their motto?

Fergal grins. 'Fire and forget.'

The European Space Centre in French Guiana was one of the many places we got into on false pretences. If anyone in there had seen five minutes of any show, we wouldn't have got within an ass's roar of the rockets, the control room and all the expensive computer gear, but Evan managed to convince them that we were a serious *Blue Peter*-type job and would treat the subject with the care and respect it deserved. The segment was all right, it was reasonably interesting, but the lads themselves were as dry as toast. Evan, in silver-tongued charmer mode, was all gracious goodbyes when we'd finished. 'Thank you so much, that was absolutely riveting, a thoroughly absorbing afternoon . . . ' For some reason, the boss of the whole place was there to see us off. 'Would you like to 'ave an informational video?' he says in his Inspector Clouseau accent. 'We can send you some stock footage of ze rocket launch that you can add into your documentary.' Our documentary. Right.

Evan, dripping charm, says. 'Oh, that would be fantastic, Monsieur. Beautiful. *Merci, merci*. Thank you again.'

As soon as we were out of earshot, I looked at Evan. 'That was shite, wasn't it.'

'Shite,' says Evan.

Rosco, all the gear slung over his shoulder, sparks up a fag. 'A load of shite.' We head back into Cayenne and go on the rip. The serious, serious rip. I mean, there's fuck all to do but drink, and the only thing to drink is this foul Kronenbourg shite. We find an old-style French bar with a pool table, and that's the end of us. At around eight in the evening, we get back to our hotel, up to my room and start on the cans.

Most of the time, the hotels are average. Every five or six countries, you'll have a fabulous five-star that Evan has managed to wrangle from the tourist board using every last drop of his Mountbellew charm. And every five or six countries, you'll have the worst kind of half-star damp shithole. Scutty little bed, little brown locker, shitty little shower with little brown rubber mat, butty portable TV on a stupid thing jutting out from the wall, no remote and four stations all in French. When this happens, as it does in French Guiana, we both turn on Evan. 'Evan, you're going to have to get serious bonus points next time.'

'Don't worry, lads, the next country, I swear to God, I swear to God, the next country you won't believe. I've got a picture of it. Look.' And that's the worst. A picture on the internet, a print-out. It looks half decent, when you get there it's nothing like that.

Evan goes through life like it's a musical, like it's *Tops of the Towns*. Beered up to the hilt in a shitty hotel room in French Guiana, he has the shirt off and is jumping around like a lunatic. 'Here, what do ye think of my tan?

'MOST OF THE TIME, THE HOTELS ARE AVERAGE. EVERY FIVE OR SIX COUNTRIES, YOU'LL HAVE A FABULOUS FIVE-STAR THAT EVAN HAS MANAGED TO WRANGLE FROM THE TOURIST BOARD USING EVERY LAST DROP OF HIS MOUNTBELLEW CHARM. **AND EVERY FIVE OR SIX COUNTRIES, YOU'LL HAVE THE WORST KIND OF HALF-STAR DAMP SHITHOLE.**'

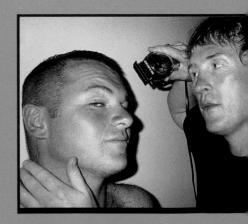

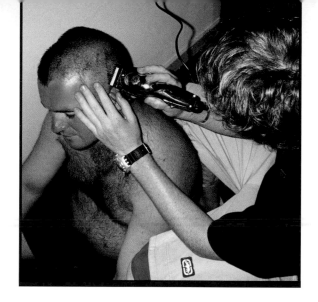

'Jeez, me hair, me hair. Me fuckin' hair is annoying the shit out of me. I think I'll get it shaved off. What do ye think? Will I get it shaved off?'

Well, Rosco has a shaver, I tell him. I'll do it for you if you like.

'Right so,' says Evan.

So we sat him down and got out the electric razor. In half a minute, he had a fine, Mohican. He goes back to leaping around the room again. 'You talkin' to me? I don't see anyone else here, you must be talking to me.' Next minute the phone rings. It's reception to say that François from the Space Agency is downstairs with the promotional video. The head of the European Space Agency is downstairs. Four hours earlier, he had met Evan Chamberlain, producer, the smooth-talking, polished professional. Now he's become a half-scuttered Travis Bickle.

Myself and Rosco collapsed on the bed. I was laughing so much I thought I was going to throw up. 'You have to go down! You have to go down!'

We never have to do any of that frontline shit, it's always Evan. He was there, 'What am I going to do?'

We pushed him out the door with the stupidest hat we could find.

Of course, typical Evan. He was down there for an hour blathering away to your man at the bar. When he came back up, he started mugging in the mirror again. 'An bhfuil tusa ag labhairt liomsa?' We let on the shaver had broke, but he wasn't having any of it. 'Stop messin', stop messin', shave the rest of it off!' We have this fascination with dead arms. You could be fast asleep, curled up on an airplane, next minute, bang, into the shoulder. The pain of it. That night, we ended up having a dead arm competition. If myself and Rosco won, the Mohican stayed. If Evan won, we shaved it off. For those who don't know, a dead arm competition works on a submission basis. You take turns to smash your opponent in the arm, and whoever decides he can't take it any more loses. Our mistake was to let Evan go first. Inside half a minute, neither myself nor Rosco could feel our fingers. When it was our turn to take revenge, the hoor didn't even flinch. So he lost the Mohican. Big white cue-ball head on him for the next week, until it turned brown.

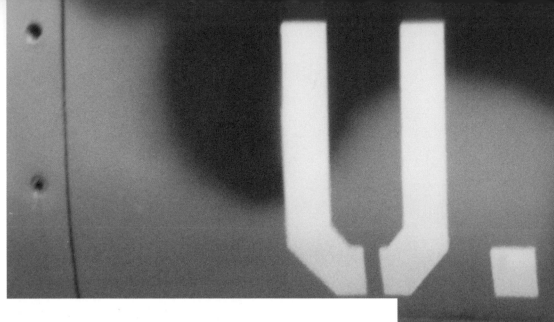

NORTH CAROLINA

NEW BERN, NORTH CAROLINA, IS A HOLE.

That's about all you need to know. Empty streets with the crappiest shops you've ever seen, full of stuff that hasn't been fashionable since the thirties. I stood staring in the window at the fine array of hairpieces on display at 'The Friendly Wig Shop' on Main Street. The town is famous, or maybe infamous, for its lost colony. A group of settlers who wandered down here in 1590 and were never seen again. I can put the mystery to rest here and now. It wasn't injuns or grizzlies that got them, it was boredom. There is nothing to do. We were staying in a Holiday Inn at a crossroads outside of town. One of the bleakest spots in the world. Every morning, I ate granola, watching the pick-ups go by outside. You'd see bumper stickers saying things like 'Charlton Heston is my President'.

This was the first *Amú* show we ever shot, also the first time I'd been to the States. We flew Dublin to Heathrow, Heathrow to Raleigh-Durham in North Carolina, then took a small plane down to New Bern, got our rental car and drove out to the Holiday Inn. That banjo riff from *Deliverance* kept playing in my head. We didn't know it at the time, but this was the first of fifty-six shows that would be shot over the coming four years, that would take me all round the world. Thank God the locations got better.

But it's in New Bern that you'll find Cherry Point Marine Base, home of the Second Marine Aircraft Wing and Marine Corps Air Station. The biggest collection of Jarheads in the world. We were here to meet Corporal Laura Boyle from Bearna i gContae na Gaillimhe.

It's like the place has been dropped from the sky into the middle of the

North Carolina countryside. One minute it's just empty road with forest running along one side, empty fields on the other. Next minute, there it is: 30,000 acres of military base, packed with something like 20,000 marines. 'Pardon our noise,' it says on the gate. 'It's the sound of freedom.'

It was like a film, like the opening shot of a war movie. We passed squadrons of marines crisscrossing the parade ground, chanting at the tops of their voices: 'I don't know but I bin told . . . ' Jeeps and cars were haring along the roads, pumping out either hip-hop or country and western. The first thing we saw once we'd cleared security was that quintessential image. Marines lowering the flag. Three of them in full ceremonial dress taking it down and squaring it away. A solitary bugle player accompanying them. In the distance, you could hear gunfire from the rifle range. But louder than any of these, the Harrier Jumpjets. Deafening. Sounding like the end of the world. Rising slowly up into the air or tearing the sky to pieces overhead. Those sonic booms going off every few minutes. It was like *Platoon* and *Full Metal Jacket* and *Hamburger Hill* and all rolled into one.

So what's a Galway girl doing stuck out in the middle of all this lunacy? Laura Boyle was working in a bar in New York when a couple of recruiting sergeants came in. She was at a loose end, the idea of soldiering appealed to her, so she signed up. Two years on, she had no regrets. Far from it. I asked her to sum up the experience in one sentence. She gave me the corps motto: 'The few, the proud, the marines.' Round the table, her buddies let out that marine cry, 'Ooraw!'

She may not be typical, but typical wasn't hard to find. I got talking to another guy, about five foot four, bald as an egg and built like a beer keg. With seventeen years' service under his belt, he had three years left to retirement. I asked him what he planned to do then. 'Gonna drink a lot of beer,' he said. 'My retirement should cover my house, my utilities, stuff like that, so I gotta get a job for beer money and food.'

Out on the assault course, the boys are showing off their tattoos: 'Only God can judge me', 'US Marine Corps', 'Semper Fidelis', 'Jake and Linda 4ever', 'The Fightin' Irish'. Marines from Tennessee and Alabama, tall and fit, all glistening, bronzed muscles and shaved heads, looking like they could eat you for breakfast. When no one's looking, I get a biro out of the glove box in Laura's car and scribble 'FCA, 33rd Batt.' at the top of my arm. What's the FCA? Everyone wants to know. Toughest of the tough, I tell them. Their motto? 'Laidir, Lively and Legless.'

'OUT ON THE ASSAULT COURSE, THE BOYS ARE SHOWING OFF THEIR TATTOOS: 'ONLY GOD CAN JUDGE ME', 'US MARINE CORPS', 'SEMPER FIDELIS', 'JAKE AND LINDA 4EVER', 'THE FIGHTIN' IRISH'. MARINES FROM TENNESSEE AND ALABAMA, TALL AND FIT, **ALL GLISTENING, BRONZED MUSCLES AND SHAVED HEADS, LOOKING LIKE THEY COULD EAT YOU FOR BREAKFAST.**'

You think obstacle courses, you think *The Krypton Factor*. I remember sitting on the couch laughing at the awkward fools who couldn't even get up that rope-net thing, or couldn't walk that simple oul beam. Lads, it's not as easy as it looks. The first obstacle was one of those high log yokes. About six foot off the ground, all you had to do was clamber up on top, swing over and off you go. In half a minute, Hector was the only one left throwing himself at it. Couldn't see the others for dust. The drill sergeant shouted himself hoarse at me. 'Get up, you pathetic, no-good, goddamn red-headed Irish freak!' I must have been a good ten minutes struggling with the thing before I gave up and walked around it. Thought that would be the worst, but I couldn't do any of the bloody course. Fell off the stupid rope-net thing. Couldn't keep my balance on the stupid beam. They had this rope you had to shinny up. Not a hope. Not a hope on the rope. By the time I finished, everyone was long gone except the lad shouting abuse, and I could barely walk.

Down on the rifle range, you've long lines of marines stretched out on the grass, aiming at targets so far away, I can't even see them. Laura takes me down to dangerous end. There, in an underground bunker, you've a whole squadron of people beavering away. The targets – each one the black silhouette of a man aiming a gun – are mounted on runners on these huge metal frames. You pull down the lever, and the target flies up above ground. The minute it gets out there, you can hear the thunk, thunk, thunk as the bullets slam into it. Down it comes again, somebody takes score, replaces the target, and back it goes.

We travelled in the back of a personnel carrier with Laura and head PR man Lieutenant Caldwell down to the furthest corner of the base, to where these two drab, semi-circular buildings sat on their own near the edge of the forest. Both covered with 'Danger, Do Not Enter' signs. On the spin down, Lt. Caldwell rang ahead to make sure they were ready for us. Did I hear him use the words 'gas chamber'?

To prepare yourself for battle situations, Laura explains, you need some experience of poisonous gas. She nods towards the smaller of the two sheds. Here's where you get it.

As we climbed down from the back of the truck, this huge, grizzled marine comes striding over. He hands me a combat jacket and a gas mask. 'You'll need these, sir.'

I'll need what?

'Sir,' he says, indicating the same shed Laura pointed out, 'this is a highly active CS gas environment, sir. If you breathe that CS gas, sir, your skin will turn purple and blotchy and you will puke like the devil.'

Ah here. Nobody said anything about any CS gas.

Laura was there, 'These masks don't let anything in. Just go in, breathe normally and you won't know anything about it.'

I didn't fancy the idea, but the cameras were rolling, and it was my first Amú gig. I couldn't back down.

The jacket he gave me was this camouflaged snorkel-type thing with a hood that fitted snugly around your head. Then the mask, fastened with straps tight to the face. Really tight, but no matter how they adjusted it, I could still feel air on exposed skin. There was myself, Laura and two other marines down there on a war-simulation exercise. In we went, first to this kind of decompression chamber, this porch on the side of the building. Over a speaker on the wall, you could hear the head lad's voice coming muffled through the hood. 'OK, soldiers, proceed to the chamber.'

Inside was dusty, derelict and poorly lit. Empty. You had that claustrophobic feeling you get when all you can hear is your own breathing, amplified now by the mask. Your man's voice again, over the speaker. 'You are now standing in a highly infected area. You cannot see the gas, you cannot smell it, but it is there . . . OK, soldiers, removing masks in ten, nine, eight . . . ' As he counted down, Laura and the other two got ready. 'Three, two, one. OK, soldiers remove masks, drop and give me ten.' I watched the three of them fall on to the bare concrete floor and race through ten of the fastest press-ups I've ever seen. When they stood up again, one of the lads had a face red as a beetroot. 'OK, soldiers, clean and replace masks.' Beetroot man's fingers are racing to do up the straps, but I can tell he hasn't lasted. He's after taking a breath. As soon as we get back out, he falls on to the grass, rips off the mask and starts puking. This awful-looking, thin white stuff.

'He'll be all right,' says Laura, not a bother on her. 'Give him an hour and he'll be fine.'

The few, the proud, the marines. Spewraw!

10 MOST BORING PLACES TO VISIT

>>> Bandar Seri Begawan, Brunei

There may be lots to do during the day, but the place keels over and dies at night. A no alcohol zone. You can bring beer in if you want, but you're only allowed drink it in the 'drinking room' of the hotel. The 'drinking room' was full of British and US ex-pats so instead we sat in my hotel room, watching CNN with a bucket of Kentucky Fried Chicken. On the plane out though, we must have got through about 150 of those miniature beer cans.

>>> Quimper, France

The worst. Fell asleep on this shitty little hobbity touristy mini-train that brings you round the town. Ate snails, did traditional dance with locals in village. Shite show. Couldn't get a cup of coffee in the afternoon.

>>> Cayenne, French Guiana

Total population: four. Highlight of our stay in the city was the time we saw a dog crossing the street. We still talk about it.

>>> Hastings

For the paranormal show, we left London at 4am to drive to Hastings. It was lashing rain and the waves were pounding the seafront. Bloody hotel wouldn't let us check-in early so I drove the car up on the footpath right in front of the doors and the three of us tried to get a couple of hours kip. Can still smell the socks.

>>> Helsinki, Finland

We told the taxi driver on the way in that we were here for five days to shoot a TV show about the place. He says that's about four days too long. Bang on the money. Reminded me of several places in Ireland. Stupid pass-the-asparagus Helly Hanson yuppie yachting hole. Too clean. Too nice. Give me Ros a Mhíl or Na Cealla Beaga any day.

>>> Hiroshima, Japan

Again, plenty to see during the day, at night, it closes up. Found a bar that charged something like €13 for a beer, so went knacker drinking. Ten minutes of the show was me standing beside closed shops, in front of railings, sitting on steps, drinking local equivalent of Buckfast out of a brown paper bag.

>>> Lima, Peru

Cat. Nothing to do. Hasn't had a drop of rain since 1974. Big sprawling soulless city centre. Head straight for Machu Picchu, don't go near Lima.

>>> New Bern, North Carolina

We were here to do the Cherry Point Marine Base show. Stayed in the first of many Holiday Inns at the junction of a motorway. In 1903, the Wright brothers made the first ever flight in New Bern. Nothing's happened since.

>>> Singapore

A city up its own arse. Can't shout on the street, can't chew gum, can't open the back window of your car. Can't understand why anyone would want to go there.

>>> Vermont, USA

Snowing. Empty. Nothing to do except every morning go down to the local drive in, get your pancakes and watch the pickups going by.

BOSTON

So when we went to check out the Big Dig in Boston during the American series, we had no problem finding Irish-speakers. The Big Dig. The largest building site in the world. One of the most ambitious civil engineering projects ever undertaken. The idea: to demolish Boston's central artery, the huge six-lane highway running through the middle of the city, and instead, dig out an immense tunnel and run the traffic through there instead. Basically, bury an entire highway. Oh yeah, and without ever shutting down the traffic. If that wasn't enough, the workers had to negotiate a maze of underground utilities: everything from sewerage to electricity, gas and water.

By the time the project was completed they had moved 16 million cubic yards of dirt in 541,000 truckloads, pumped in 3.8 million cubic yards of concrete and used enough reinforcing steel to encircle the planet. In among the 5,000 workers, you had hundreds of Irish, who consumed 7.5 million breakfast rolls, 9.3 million cups of tea and drank enough porter in the evening to flood the entire project seven times over. There were 1,432 pairs of fluorescent wellies, 685 semi-visible arse cracks and 851 arguments over who stole me mug.

I've had conversations in Irish in a lot of strange places, but maybe this was the strangest. In a Portakabin 120 feet below the streets of Boston, with a handful of the 200 Connemara boys working on the project. These lads were typical builders. Up on the streets above us, the dig had the city up in a heap. There were hoardings and diversions everywhere, and traffic was bumper to bumper more or less all the time. 'Ah, tá siad happy enough,' says Jimmy McDonagh with a dismissive wave of his hand.

He talks about the elevated highway that the tunnel will replace. 'Sure, bhi sé réidh le titim anyway.' This is the Irish of Connemara builders. You'll hear nothing like it anywhere else.

Boys, we'll have to pour that raft today

Leaids, caithfimíd an raft a phouráil inniú

That machine pumps the concrete

Pumpáileann said an concrete leis an machine sin

We'll reinforce that steel, lads

Reinforcáilimid an steel sin leaids

My bike is broken

Tá mo bhicycle shagálta

Jimmy's been on site for seven years. Though he looks as though he's shovelled at least 16 million cubic yards of dirt in his time, he has now swapped the shovel for a walkie-talkie. He takes me on a tour of the site – his site – past skips with Sinn Féin graffiti and lads who nod respectfully to him as we walk by. Despite those seven years, he's lost nothing of the Connemara accent. He tells me about the unions. Local 223 is for the Connemara boys. 'Bionn said ag representáil na workers.'

These days, of course, the Paddies aren't just the lads with the hard hats and the blisters. Sean O'Neil from Ennis in County Clare is head of PR with the project. 'The difference is dramatic,' he says. 'The Irish that came over fifty years ago wouldn't be supervising. Now they're running the place. You've got instrumentation specialists, design specialists, co-ordinators, architects . . . Education, that's what did it, which means better money, which means more stability. They can get jobs with Bechtel – the main contractor for the entire thing. They do little jobs like rebuilding Kuwait.'

Despite what the Connemara boys said, muintir Boston aren't that thrilled with a project that's been going for the bones of ten years. 'We had one fella jumped over a wall here one time,' says Sean. 'He just started running around throwing shit. He was in a car and he was stuck in traffic and he just snapped. He started fucking out everybody. About nine guys came over and threw him back over the wall again.'

IF YOU WANT TO DIG A SERIOUSLY BIG HOLE, YOU'RE GOING TO HAVE TO GET THE IRISH INVOLVED. THERE'S NO NATION ON EARTH WITH MORE EXPERIENCE OF THE SHOVEL. SO WHEN WE WENT TO CHECK OUT THE BIG DIG IN BOSTON DURING THE AMERICAN SERIES, WE HAD NO PROBLEM FINDING IRISH-SPEAKERS. THE BIG DIG. THE LARGEST BUILDING SITE IN THE WORLD.

NEW YORK

WHAT'S THE BEST WAY TO GET AROUND NEW YORK? CAB? SUBWAY? NEITHER. YOU WANT TO SEE THE REAL BIG APPLE, GET YOURSELF A POLICE ESCORT.

We were in town for the last show of the American tour. Of all the series we've done, this one – the first – was by far the most gruelling. Eighteen flights and ten programmes in thirty-five days. In Asia and South America, we only shot three more shows but had three months to do it. By the time we got to New York, we were almost burnt out. But, coming in by cab from JFK, the sight of that skyline, the buzz coming off the place, and suddenly we got a new burst of energy. First thing, I went down to Times Square and queued up to get into the David Letterman audience. It was gas. Up on the big screen in front of the set, they've these instructions flashing up the whole time. 'Clap', 'Clap Louder', 'Laugh', 'Roar'. Disobey and you're out on your ear.

On the way back to the hotel, I caught sight of a poster for one of my favourite bands, the Charlatans. They were playing that night in this small Olympia-type venue with the Stereophonics. We managed to blag our way in, saying we were these big, important dudes from Irish TV.

Back then, the shows were based around Irish-speakers in quirky or interesting jobs, and our main story in New York was Paul McCormack. From Ballybofey in County Donegal, he was an Irish-speaker and, at twenty-nine years old, the youngest-ever police captain in the NYPD. He'd emigrated back in the bad old days of the late eighties, worked in construction for a bit, then joined the force in 1990. Ten years later, he was commanding officer of the thirty-third precinct.

The first morning, Paul came by to our hotel to collect us for an interview with the chief of patrol, a second-generation Paddy called John Scanlon. Scanlon was your

typical Irish cop. Up on the 700th floor of police headquarters, John's office was decked out in memorabilia and photos of himself with the likes of Ronald Reagan, Nelson Mandela and Kofi Annan. I asked him if it was Scanlon or Scanlan, and he let out this big laugh. 'You're just like my uncle Tommy back home in Ireland.' We talked a bit about Giuliani and how the crime rate had tumbled in the city in the last few years. As we left, he says to Paul, 'Get this guy anything he wants. Speedboat ride up the Brooklyn river? Helicopter? You make sure he gets it.'

Cool.

Paul took us down to his neighbourhood, to the headquarters of the thirty-third. It was like walking on to the set of any New York cop show you've ever seen. Big, fat desk sergeant scowling at everyone behind the counter, Latin American prostitute in a tiny miniskirt arguing in Spanish, huge black guy getting fingerprinted. McCormack, only about five foot six but tough as fuck, spoke Irish in this heavy Bronx accent. You'd have to listen very carefully to hear any trace of Donegal. He had all these medals stacked up on his lapel. One for each time he'd faced down an armed criminal.

'LADS, DO YE WANT TO GO DOWN TO THE EMPIRE STATE BUILDING?' IT'S ABOUT FORTY-FIVE MINUTES THROUGH THE TRAFFIC FOR EVERYONE ELSE, BUT MICK JUST TURNS ON THE LOUDSPEAKER ON THE ROOF OF THE CAR. **ALL THE WAY DOWN FIFTH AVENUE, YOU CAN HEAR THIS HEAVY DUBLIN ACCENT SINGING OUT: 'NYPD. GER OURRA THE WAY, WILL YIZ?'**

In the afternoon, he took us on a drugs bust. Sitting in the van three blocks south of where the thing was to go down, Paul explained that a SNU (Special Narcotics Unit) team had been following this guy for the past weeks and that today, they intended to bring him in. They had teams of undercover cops in place all round the spot where your man dealt, and whole squadrons of uniformed lads ready to swoop once the word came in. We sat for ages in the van, listening to the different teams talking to each other over the radio. 'Guy in a black cap walking south on Amsterdam from 159. Wait 'til I give the word, then grab him.' At the signal, Paul hits the siren on the van and off we go. Tearing down through the traffic to where the cops already have two guys in cuffs. One spread-eagled against the wall, another up against a car. The first guy, the dealer, had been selling cocaine and crack cocaine out of the engine of his car. The second guy, well dressed and sophisticated-looking, was just the unfortunate, poor bastard who happened to be buying when the cops swooped. Back at the thirty-third, they haul the two guys in and book 'em, just like on the movies.

And just like in the movies, all the boys can talk about now is food. Mick Corridan, from Rathfarnham, another cop based in the thirty-third, takes myself and Paul out for Philly cheese steaks.

For the rest of our stay, Mick's on hand to take us wherever we want to go. 'Lads, do ye want to go down to the Empire State Building?' It's about forty-five minutes through the traffic for everyone else, but Mick just turns on the loudspeaker on the roof of the car. All the way down Fifth Avenue, you can hear this heavy Dublin accent singing out: 'NYPD. Ger ourra the way, will yiz?' It's like the parting of the Red Sea as the lines of yellow cabs dodge left and right. We're down there in ten minutes. Class.

'I MET WESTLIFE IN SEOUL ON THE ASIAN TRIP AND THE DUBLINERS A COUPLE OF YEARS LATER IN VIENNA. BOTH ARE FOND OF THE BALLADS, OF COURSE, EXCEPT THAT YOU DON'T HEAR TOO MUCH ABOUT MURDER, WHISKEY OR NAVVYING IN WESTLIFE SONGS, WHICH IS AN AWFUL SHAME. A FEW WHACK FOL DE DIDDLE AYE DOS IN THE LIKES OF 'MANDY' OR 'YOU RAISE ME UP' WOULD IMPROVE THEM NO END,'

VIENNA AND SEOUL

WESTLIFE AND THE DUBLINERS. Two of our most successful musical exports. I met Westlife in Seoul on the Asian trip and the Dubliners a couple of years later in Vienna. Both are fond of the ballads, of course, except that you don't hear too much about murder, whiskey or navvying in Westlife songs, which is an awful shame. A few whack fol de diddle aye dos in the likes of 'Mandy' or 'You Raise Me Up' would improve them no end.

There's no folkie as hardcore as an Austrian folkie. It might be a mild spring evening in Vienna, but there's dozens of bawneen jumpers among the 600-odd crowd. Plenty of denim caps, moccasins and almost as much facial hair as there is up on stage. Original seventies Lisdoonvarna t-shirts, tricolours, the faint smell of lentils. You can be pretty sure that half the people here have survived cycling holidays up along the west coast or spent six months in a cottage in Killaloe.

The first night, I get to introduce the boys, and they wander on to the stage like brickies on to a site. No pyrotechnics, no spandex, no dry ice. Barney doesn't skid in on his knees or start playing the banjo with his teeth. No one's in any hurry.

Looking back out through the wings, the ranged beards of the Dubliners is some sight. You can't see much of Barney between the grey-black mane and the cap, except the little eyes twinkling behind the glasses. Beside him, fiddle man John Sheahan's got a tight, clean beard, the kind that Santy might wear during the summer. Then you've Sean Cannon with a neat ginger leprechaun effort. Paddy Reilly is the non-believer, the only man in the band who knows how to use a razor. Last in line, Eamonn Campbell looks like the wild man of Borneo. He makes up for Paddy's lack of faith with a wild mess of hair halfway between candyfloss and gorse.

ATHAS AN DOMHAIN BUALADH
LEAT, A HÉCTOR.
LE GACH DEA-GHUÍ. Seán Cannon

Never mind the width
feel the "Quality"
To Hector
"ya Boy ya" · **the Dubliners**

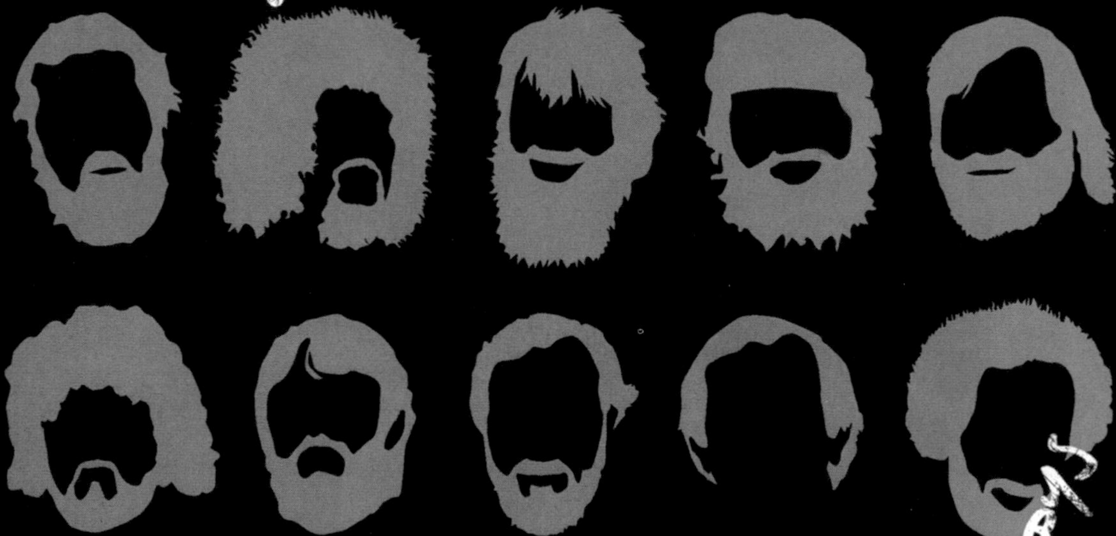

Do HECTOR.
SLÁINTE MHIÉ
GO BRÁ.
BARNEY.

Pat Reilly
Up the Rebel

NEVER FORGET
THE BOGEY BOYS

official tour programme

Just as they're about to strike up, you could hear a pin drop. Total reverence. Back home, a Dubliners gig can get fairly rowdy. Everyone scuttered, singing along whether they know the words or not. In Vienna, no one so much as whispers until the band invites the crowd to sing. Then they respond as if they've all been getting together every Tuesday night for the last six months to practise. They know every word of every song.

Seven nights, seven gigs. The place sold out each night. Because the band's been coming here regularly since the mid-seventies, Vienna has become a second home for them. Now the Austrians are recognizing that fact officially. On the Wednesday, the band is due in the Rathaus – the town hall – to receive the Rathausmann. It's the equivalent of the freedom of the city. We're here for the week, to hang around with the band and get a flavour of what it's like to be a member of the Irish equivalent of the Rolling Stones.

The first night, you'd be forgiven for thinking that it was the Rolling Stones we were with. Groupies crowd the stage door, old friends they've gotten to know over the years are all backstage, chatting with the boys. The whiskey, wine and Kombucha are flowing. Everyone's in flying form. John Sheahan is talking about the line-up changes they've had over the years. 'Takes a while to get used to a sound like that missing, Ronnie Drew's voice, but I suppose we were fortunate persuading Paddy Reilly to join.' Despite the fact that Paddy had been with the band for something like eight years, he was still a relative newcomer. And, of course, his reputation had been made long before he got involved with the boys. The following day, he explains how he came to release *that* song. 'Myself and Eamonn Campbell had just finished recording an album. The Barleycorn had already had the song out. They released it and it went

The Dubliners' Rider

BACKSTAGE AT A DUBLINERS GIG, THE PROMOTER IS REQUIRED TO PROVIDE THE FOLLOWING:

> **Two bottles of Black Bush whiskey**

> **One six-pack of beer**

> **Two bottles of red wine**

> **Two bottles of Kombucha**

> **Six litres of mineral water**

to number ten or twelve in the charts. Jim Hand, who unfortunately has since left us, said, 'That's the one, Paddy.' I said, 'There's no point bringing out "The Fields of Athenry", the Barleycorn have already had it out.' He said, 'I don't care, that's the one.' Sure, it went through the roof in a matter of weeks.'

Eamonn is head axe-man, the Slash of the Dubliners. Over a few pints, he tells me that he actually started his musical career on the accordion. But then came the fateful day when he heard Elvis on the radio for the first time. 'Fuck the accordion,' I said, 'I want a guitar, Mammy, I want a guitar!'

The night before we're due in the town hall, the boys are brave enough to allow me on stage to sing 'The Wild Rover' with them, and afterwards, we head across the road to the pub. Of course, instead of getting an early night, one pint turns into two, and two becomes two dozen. They may have about four hundred years between them, but the Dubliners are still well capable of tearing the arse out of it. It's not long before the singing starts, and at one point all six of us are sitting there, eyes closed, one finger in the ear, doing the close harmonies on 'The Auld Triangle'. At about five in the morning, after working our way through every song in the Dubliners' songbook, we stumble out of the restaurant and head home.

Sweet suffering Jesus, I thought I was going to die the next day. I'm standing in line with the band in the opulent interior of the Rathaus while the Deputy Mayor gives her spiel. As I look down the line, the massed beards of the Dubliners seem seriously out of place. You've uniformed servants standing to attention, huge gold columns, high walls hung with massive paintings. There are long mahogany tables laden with magnums of champagne, silver trays of hors d'œuvres, prawns and caviar. Big pyramids of Ferrero Rocher . . . This is about as far from O'Donoghue's on Merrion Row as it gets. I've got the usual mixture of sweats and shakes, with the cloigeann tinn on top. The boys, though, look none the worse for wear. Maybe they weren't lowering as much Austrian beer as I was, maybe they make a better fist of hiding it, maybe they're just too hard. Call that a piss-up? That wasn't a piss-up! At the end of the ceremony, they all sit down and start playing, not a bother on them. True pros.

Seven men in suits meet us at the airport in Seoul. A couple from the tourist board, a couple from the Ministry for Foreign Affairs and three more we never manage to identify. They stand at the arrivals gate clustered round a large sign that says simply 'Hector'.

The head of the delegation is full of welcomes, but he makes no attempt to introduce the rest of them. As we head out to meet the van, they all follow. Rosco is still dying from the food poisoning we picked up at the Great Wall. Myself and Evan are over the worst of it, but Rosco has spent most of the flight from China in the jacks, groaning softly to himself and making the back seats of the plane pretty much unusable. Outside the terminal building, our Hiace is waiting. Evan turns to say thanks and goodbye to the reception party, but they're all filing past him into the van. Rosco, who's already climbed in and curled up in the back, is forced to make more and more room as this procession of Koreans piles in beside him. As soon as we get moving, he sits up and, in his best Father Jack, says to Evan: 'Who the fuck are these people?' Evan shrugs. 'Haven't a clue.'

In the hotel, we split up. Evan heads downtown for a look around; I settle in to watch a movie while, in the room next to mine, Rosco gets back to groaning. An hour later, the phone rings. Evan. 'Guess what. Westlife is playing in the basketball arena around the corner.'

No way.

'Yep. Tonight for one night only. Will I see if I can get us in to see them?'

Evan, if you can get us in there and Rosco is able for it, we'll do it.

A couple of hours later, we're downtown, walking past endless rows of Korean teeny boppers. There's about eight thousand of them, lined up in the most orderly queue I've ever seen, two abreast like they're about to walk into the ark. Once we've negotiated security and the many handlers and media people, we're shown into the backstage room where the boys are lounging, eating burgers and chips, dressed in white suits and looking like they're just after getting in from school.

So straight away, I start into my Irish class. Suigh síos a bhuacaillí agus dún do bhéal. Is mise an múinteoir and tá ceisteanna agam daoibh. McFadden isn't having any of it. He's up and off and stays in the background the whole time we're there, going on about his stupid, fuckin' Irish teacher . . . Shane and Mark got into it though and we had some fun with them, dredging their memories for the cúpla focail. Cian stayed interested for a bit, but then, when he couldn't answer a single question, he got all sulky and clammed up completely. I grabbed a few posters from the press office and got them all to sign one for the missus and one for the mother. My mother loves Westlife. She still has hers up on her bedroom wall. 'To Trina, love you always. Bryan, Cian, Nicky, Shane and Mark.'

The stage manager comes bounding in and announces there's two minutes to go. So I gather the boys together and give them the usual motivational speech.

Now, lads, this is what all the training is for, all dem cold nights in January where ye sweated yer bollix off. Now, lads, yiz are well able to play, I want ye to get out there and sing yer little hearts out. This is more than a jersey, boys, I want ye to get out there and make us proud!

A little slap on the arse and off they went.

A FINAL CAUTIONARY TALE

A FEW WEEKS INTO THE ASIA TRIP, WE ALL STARTED COLLECTING STUFF. It was kind of inevitable. There was so much great gear to be had, from fake designer clothes to art to antiques, and it was all dirt cheap. The only problem was hauling it around. By the time we got to Japan – the last stop – we had a total of seventeen bags between us. Rosco had all the camera gear of course and I'd everything from cushion covers to chopsticks to fake runners. Evan was after developing a fascination with musical instruments and had all kinds of mandolins and drums hanging off him.

Anyway. We wrapped up the second-last show in Kyoto and got a speed train down to Tokyo to shoot the last one. When we arrived at the station, there were no baggage trolleys and we had to pull and drag all seventeen bags up six different escalators by hand. It was like something out of a bad sitcom. Evan there in his Koh Samui singlet and flip-flops chasing runaway baggage as it tumbled back down the steps.

We were due home at the end of the week. The twenty-second flight of the trip would be with KLM to Amsterdam, and from there we would make a connection to Dublin. Travelling with all that accumulated stuff was such an ordeal, we decided that on the day of our flight home, nothing would be left to chance. Nothing.

The plane was due to take-off at eleven-thirty. We were in Narita airport, at the top of the check-in queue at seven a.m.

The desk opened at eight. Three and a half hours to the flight. One by one, we tagged the bags and put them through, then watched them disappear off down the carousel and through the hatch. All smiles, the girl checked my passport, then Rosco's and issued us both with boarding cards. Great. All set. We sauntered off down towards the gate while Evan finished up at the desk. Rosco had this stupid little rubber ball that he was firing around the place. When we got to passport control, I looked back and Evan was still at the desk, so myself and Rosco started messing around with the ball, waiting for him.

'Come on,' says Rosco after a bit, 'we'll go to the duty free.' Fair enough says I, but before we leave, I glance back towards check-in. We're fifty yards away but I can see from Evan's body language that something's wrong. He's got his arms open, he's standing back from the desk. Rosco's about to hand over his boarding card when I tell him to hang on a second. Evan turns and looks over at us. He starts making frantic 'get back here' gestures.

Excess baggage charges. They wanted £3,500. Three Thousand Five Hundred Irish Pounds. Your one was about to issue Evan with his card when somebody came running over, telling her to wait. We were about two hundred kilos over.

The desk had opened at eight. At half nine, we were still standing there, arguing.

This is lunacy. You could buy a car for £3,500. We're not paying.

Then you're not getting on the plane.

Yes we are.

No you're not.

Yes we bloody well are.

No you're bloody well not.

We went through three different check-in people, two supervisors and a manager. They wouldn't give an inch.

At half ten, a hour from take off, they insisted we remove our bags from the plane. Accompanied by two security guards and a KLM rep, I went down an elevator, through the staff quarters, then out through a tunnel to the baggage holding area. One by one, I had to pick out the bags. That one there, that one, that one...

At ten forty-five, we were back in front of the desk, dragging clothes out of bags and trying to cram them into hand luggage. Stuff was even going in the bin, but no matter how we worked it, there were always at least seven bags over. We'd either have to ditch them or miss the plane. After three months of travelling, we were all homesick and exhausted. We'd been looking forward to getting this flight for weeks. There was no way on earth we were going to miss this plane. So what the hell are we going to do with these seven bags? There's the post office over there, says the girl. Nothing else for it. Sweating like pigs, watching the seconds tick down, we put in ten frantic minutes moving stuff around between the bags, sealing them and handing them over at the post office. It cost us £350 each to mail the seven stupid bags.

Back to the desk. Right, you're clear. With three heavy pieces of hand luggage each, we started running. At eleven twenty-five, we were tearing across the tarmac on to the waiting bus. I could see the plane in the distance, the only KLM among a line of Singapore Airlines 747s. The bus-driver was there, 'Where have you been? Come on! Come on!'

He drove to the wrong fucking plane. There wasn't even a gangway up to it.

Now the hoor starts dragging his heels. Off we go again, heartbreakingly slowly, stopping to let all these stupid little trolleys and tractors go by. Eleven thirty-five, lathered in sweat, looking like shit, broken mandolins and bits of ethnic Thai art hanging out of fake designer bags, we're clambering up the steps. The head flight attendant is standing at the top. Like all KLM staff: blond, tanned and Dutch. Immaculate in his blue uniform, not a hair out of place. He fixes Evan with this bitchy stare. 'Mr Chamberlain. If you ever do that to a KLM flight again, you will never board another flight with us.'

Now the walk of shame, past rows and rows of tut-tutting Dutch people to our seats, way down the back. Three dozy Irish gimps after delaying a 747 with 400 plus people on board.

I plonk down in the middle seat. Oh, sweet Jesus. We're here. That was shite, says I.

'Shite,' says Evan.

Rosco, closing his eyes. 'Shite.'

THANKS TO

dympna mi mujer - mi mejor amiga - te quiero xxxx

BHÍ [ANSEO

JOHN HEARNE,
a big fan of the show right
from the beginning
my 'write hand man'

Sarah Fraser @ Penguin uk

MEAS MÓR

Morie, Lily and Tom X

BIG SHOUT OUT TO LOCKEY'S PUB

I ♥ Navan

COLÁISTE NA bhFiann

ALL IN BAREFIELD!

THE CUL

RICHARD AND EANAN @ LISA RICHARDS

AD CRIÚ AR FAD @ T4

UP THE ROYALS!!

Scoil Mhuire Navan

NEVER
FONZY... 4GET... BADGER
YA

Faith O'Grady
for her Faith

THE BROS

Roy Keane - Red Legend

So deo!

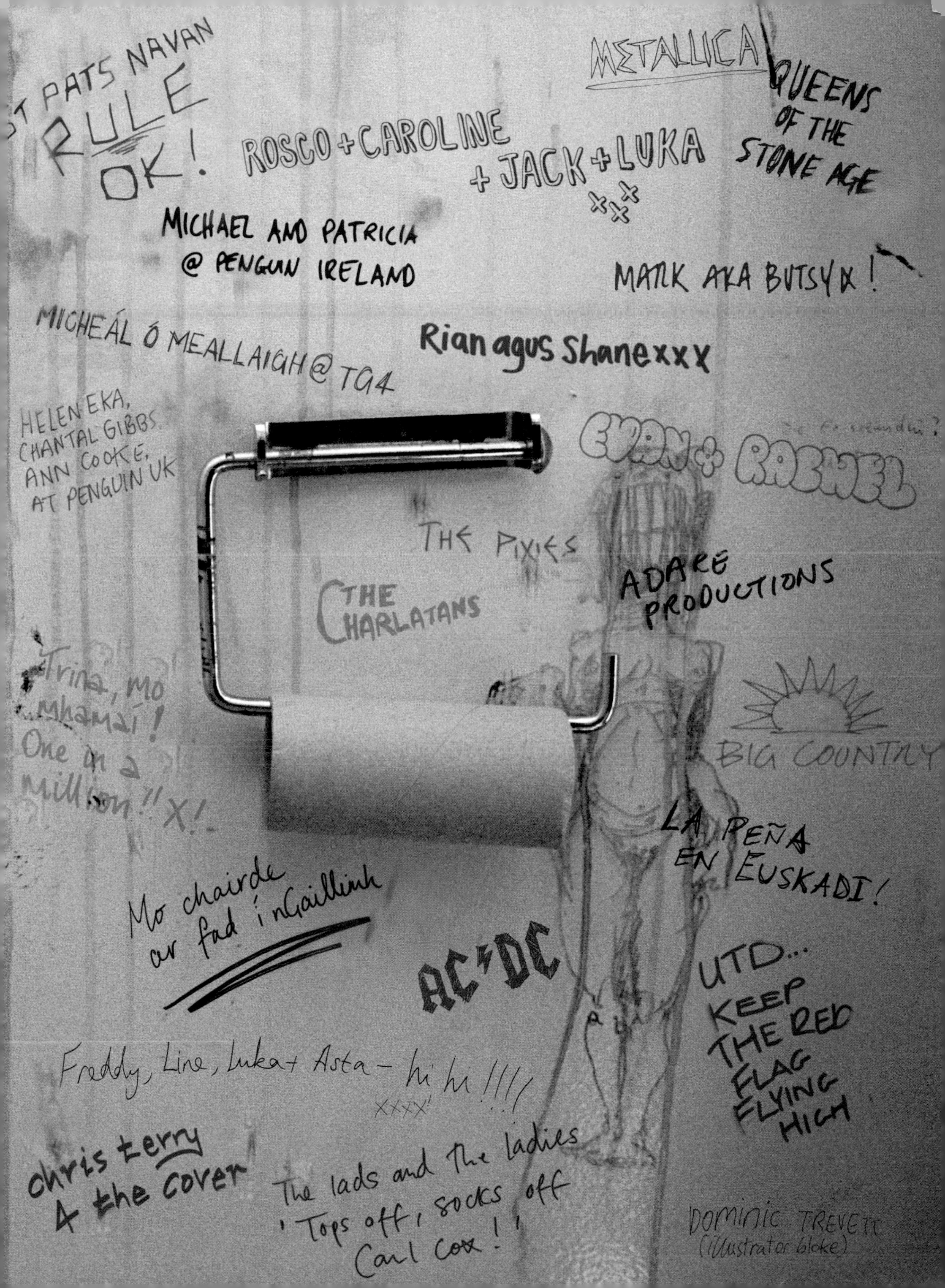

ST PATS NAVAN
RULE
OK !

ROSCO + CAROLINE
+ JACK + LUKA
x x

METALLICA
QUEENS
OF THE
STONE AGE

MICHAEL AND PATRICIA
@ PENGUIN IRELAND

MARK AKA BUTSY x !

MICHEÁL Ó MEALLAIGH @ TG4

Rian agus Shane xxx

HELEN EKA,
CHANTAL GIBBS,
ANN COOKE,
AT PENGUIN UK

EVAN + RACHEL

THE PIXIES

THE CHARLATANS

ADARE PRODUCTIONS

BIG COUNTRY

Trina, mo
mhamaí !
One in a
Million !! X !

LA PEÑA
EN EUSKADI !

Mo chairde
ar fad i nGaillimh

AC/DC

UTD...
KEEP
THE RED
FLAG
FLYING
HIGH

Freddy, Line, Luka + Asta — hi hi !!!!
xxxx

Chris Terry
4 the Cover

The lads and The ladies
'Tops off, socks off
Carl Cox ! '

DOMINIC TREVETT
(Illustrator bloke)

Slán tamall a chairde. . .